SRA Real Math

Stephen S. Willoughby

Carl Bereiter

Peter Hilton

Joseph H. Rubinstein

Joan Moss

Jean Pedersen

SRA

Columbus, OH

The **McGraw·Hill** Companies

Problem Solving

The United States government studied playground safety and determined the appropriate heights of guardrails.

Minimum Height of Playground Guardrails

The minimum height of a guardrail should prevent the largest child from inadvertently falling over the guardrail. In addition, the guardrail should extend low enough to prevent the smallest child from inadvertently going under it.

A. 29-inch minimum for pre-school-age children
   38-inch minimum for school-age children

B. 23-inch maximum for preschool-age children
   28-inch maximum for school-age children

Source: U.S. Consumer Product Safety Commission

Imagine you are designing a playground for children ages 2 to 10. The playground has a raised platform with a guardrail. Work in groups to answer the following questions.

1. How high above the platform can the bottom of the guardrail be?

2. How high above the platform can the top of the guardrail be?

3. In your design, what will be the distance from the bottom of the guardrail to the top? Explain your decision.

Multidigit Addition

Key Ideas

Adding multidigit numbers is similar to the adding you have done so far.

Sean orders a slice of pizza and a garden salad with dressing. The salad has 225 calories. The pizza has 389 calories. Add to find the total number of calories in Sean's meal.

Add: $225 + 389 = ?$

Two numbers are added together to get a sum.

Where do we start when adding multidigit numbers? Why?

Here's how:

$$\begin{array}{r} 1 \\ 225 \\ +\,389 \\ \hline 4 \end{array}$$

Start at the right. Add the ones. $5 + 9 = 14$
There are 14 ones, so we can say
$14 = 1$ ten and 4 ones.

You can write 1 above the tens column to remind yourself to add 1, or you can just remember to add it as you start the next column to the left.

$$\begin{array}{r} 11 \\ 225 \\ +\,389 \\ \hline 14 \end{array}$$

Add the tens. $1 + 2 + 8 = 11$
There are 11 tens, so we can say
11 tens $= 1$ hundred and 1 ten.

$$\begin{array}{r} 11 \\ 225 \\ +\,389 \\ \hline 614 \end{array}$$

Add the hundreds. $1 + 2 + 3 = 6$
There are 6 hundreds.
Sean's meal has 614 calories.

If we had started on the left, we would have added 2 and 3 and written 5 in the hundreds column. Then when we added 2 and 8, we would have gotten 10, and would have to write 0 in the tens column and change the 5 in the hundreds column to 6. Finally, when we added 5 and 9 in the ones column, we would get 14. We would have to write 4 in the ones column and change the 0 in the tens column to 1. Starting at the right is easier!

Here is another example.

11	Add the ones. $7 + 2 + 6 = 15$ ones =
237	1 ten and 5 ones.
592	Add the tens. $1 + 3 + 9 + 0 = 13$ tens =
+ 806	1 hundred and 3 tens.
1,635	Add the hundreds. $1 + 2 + 5 + 8 =$
	16 hundreds = 1 thousand and 6 hundreds.

Add. Use shortcuts when you can.

1
$$\begin{array}{r} 35 \\ + 42 \\ \hline \end{array}$$

2
$$\begin{array}{r} 25 \\ + 25 \\ \hline \end{array}$$

3
$$\begin{array}{r} 75 \\ + 75 \\ \hline \end{array}$$

4
$$\begin{array}{r} 62 \\ + 78 \\ \hline \end{array}$$

5
$$\begin{array}{r} 500 \\ + 500 \\ \hline \end{array}$$

6
$$\begin{array}{r} 500 \\ + 499 \\ \hline \end{array}$$

7
$$\begin{array}{r} 499 \\ + 499 \\ \hline \end{array}$$

8
$$\begin{array}{r} 562 \\ + 31 \\ \hline \end{array}$$

9
$$\begin{array}{r} 5712 \\ + 6314 \\ \hline \end{array}$$

10
$$\begin{array}{r} 89341 \\ + 10659 \\ \hline \end{array}$$

11
$$\begin{array}{r} 4315 \\ + 2690 \\ \hline \end{array}$$

12
$$\begin{array}{r} 323759902 \\ + 474621326 \\ \hline \end{array}$$

13
$$\begin{array}{r} 35 \\ 63 \\ + 75 \\ \hline \end{array}$$

14
$$\begin{array}{r} 19 \\ 25 \\ 36 \\ + 143 \\ \hline \end{array}$$

15
$$\begin{array}{r} 25 \\ 25 \\ 25 \\ + 25 \\ \hline \end{array}$$

16
$$\begin{array}{r} 250 \\ 250 \\ 250 \\ + 250 \\ \hline \end{array}$$

17
$$\begin{array}{r} 17 \\ 26 \\ + 138 \\ \hline \end{array}$$

18
$$\begin{array}{r} 32 \\ 47 \\ + 64 \\ \hline \end{array}$$

19
$$\begin{array}{r} 26 \\ 26 \\ 26 \\ + 26 \\ \hline \end{array}$$

20
$$\begin{array}{r} 33 \\ 33 \\ + 34 \\ \hline \end{array}$$

You can often tell whether an answer could be correct without working the problem out on paper. Discuss the following calculations from Jensen's TV Store.

Jensen's TV Store

ITEM	COST
M2117 Television	$375.62
Tax	26.29
Total	$638.52

Choose each correct answer.

In each of the following problems, two of the answers do not make sense, and one is correct.

21 49 + 49 = ☐

   a. 98

   b. 198

   c. 518

24 27 + 54 = ☐

   a. 81

   b. 31

   c. 171

27 412 + 562 = ☐

   a. 974

   b. 1,274

   c. 774

30 1,379 + 1,682 = ☐

   a. 4,061

   b. 2,061

   c. 3,061

22 84 + 120 = ☐

   a. 204

   b. 34

   c. 974

25 48 + 71 = ☐

   a. 199

   b. 319

   c. 119

28 73 + 793 = ☐

   a. 766

   b. 1,066

   c. 866

31 4,778 + 173 = ☐

   a. 951

   b. 4,951

   c. 4,751

23 125 + 237 = ☐

   a. 1,762

   b. 198

   c. 362

26 359 + 982 = ☐

   a. 1,041

   b. 1,341

   c. 941

29 1,475 + 325 = ☐

   a. 800

   b. 1,800

   c. 2,800

32 7,253 + 347 = ☐

   a. 10,600

   b. 7,000

   c. 7,600

ⓔ **Textbook** This lesson is available in the *eTextbook*.

Game

Addition and Strategies Practice

Don't Go Over 1,000 Game

Players: Two or more

Materials: *Number Cubes:* two 0–5 (red), two 5–10 (blue)

Object: To get the sum closest to, but not over, 1,000

Math Focus: Place value, multidigit addition, and mathematical reasoning

HOW TO PLAY

1 Roll all four **Number Cubes**. If you roll a 10, roll that cube again.

2 Combine three of the rolled numbers to make a three-digit number. You may start numbers with zeros.

3 Roll all four cubes again. Make a second three-digit number and add it to your first number.

4 You may stop after your second roll, or you may roll again, make another three-digit number, and add it to your previous sum. You can roll as many times as you like.

5 The player whose sum is closest to, but not over, 1,000 is the winner.

SAMPLE GAME

Megan rolled:

5	4	3	6
3	6	7	2

Megan stopped.

Megan wrote:

$$\begin{array}{r} 643 \\ + 327 \\ \hline 970 \end{array}$$

Rosalie rolled:

0	5	9	1
3	7	7	1
8	2	3	9

Rosalie wrote:

$$\begin{array}{r} 519 \\ + 137 \\ \hline 656 \\ + 329 \\ \hline 985 \end{array}$$

Rosalie was the winner.

 **Journal**

Explain your strategy for playing the **Don't Go Over 1,000 Game.**

Multidigit Subtraction

Key Ideas

To subtract, you may need to regroup.

Trini sold 594 tickets for the spring music festival. She sold 378 adult tickets. The rest were children's tickets.

How many children's tickets did Trini sell?

Subtract: 594 − 378 = ▨

$$\begin{array}{r} 594 \\ -378 \end{array}$$
When one number is subtracted from another number, the result is called the **difference**.

Where do we start? Why?

$$\begin{array}{r} 594 \\ -378 \end{array}$$
Subtract the ones.
You can't subtract 8 from 4.

$$\begin{array}{r} {\small 8\ 14} \\ 5\cancel{9}\cancel{4} \\ -\ 378 \end{array}$$
Regroup the 9 tens and 4 ones.

$$\begin{array}{r} {\small 8\ 14} \\ 5\cancel{9}\cancel{4} \\ -\ 378 \\ \hline 6 \end{array}$$
Subtract the ones.
14 − 8 = 6

$$\begin{array}{r} {\small 8\ 14} \\ 5\cancel{9}\cancel{4} \\ -\ 378 \\ \hline 16 \end{array}$$
Subtract the tens.
8 − 7 = 1
There is 1 ten.

$$\begin{array}{r} {\small 8\ 14} \\ 5\cancel{9}\cancel{4} \\ -\ 378 \\ \hline 216 \end{array}$$
Subtract the hundreds.
5 − 3 = 2
There are 2 hundreds.

Trini sold 216 children's tickets.

Note: You may do the regrouping without crossing off digits and writing regrouped symbols above if you wish.

e Textbook This lesson is available in the *eTextbook*.

$$\begin{array}{r} 905 \\ -\ 466 \\ \hline \end{array}$$

What do you do in a case like this?
There are no tens to regroup.

$$\begin{array}{r} 89\ 15 \\ \cancel{905} \\ -\ 466 \\ \hline 439 \end{array}$$

In this problem 9 hundreds is the same as 90 tens.
Regroup 90 tens and 5 ones.
90 tens and 5 ones = 89 tens and 15 ones

$$\begin{array}{r} 89\ 15 \\ \cancel{905} \\ -\ 466 \\ \hline 439 \end{array}$$

Now subtract.

Subtract. Use shortcuts when you can.

1 $35 - 23 = \blacksquare$

2 $65 - 29 = \blacksquare$

3 $47 - 40 = \blacksquare$

4 $47 - 39 = \blacksquare$

5 $93 - 87 = \blacksquare$

6 $425 - 425 = \blacksquare$

7
$$\begin{array}{r} 691 \\ -\ 25 \\ \hline \end{array}$$

8
$$\begin{array}{r} 201 \\ -\ 187 \\ \hline \end{array}$$

9
$$\begin{array}{r} 905 \\ -\ 377 \\ \hline \end{array}$$

10
$$\begin{array}{r} 391 \\ -\ 280 \\ \hline \end{array}$$

11
$$\begin{array}{r} 276 \\ -\ 137 \\ \hline \end{array}$$

12
$$\begin{array}{r} 672 \\ -\ 314 \\ \hline \end{array}$$

13
$$\begin{array}{r} 6542 \\ -\ 3000 \\ \hline \end{array}$$

14
$$\begin{array}{r} 1000 \\ -\ 3 \\ \hline \end{array}$$

15
$$\begin{array}{r} 218700399 \\ -\ 34969721 \\ \hline \end{array}$$

Add or subtract. Use shortcuts when you can.

16
$$\begin{array}{r} 871 \\ -\ 645 \\ \hline \end{array}$$

17
$$\begin{array}{r} 700 \\ -\ 200 \\ \hline \end{array}$$

18
$$\begin{array}{r} 700 \\ +\ 200 \\ \hline \end{array}$$

19
$$\begin{array}{r} 700 \\ -\ 199 \\ \hline \end{array}$$

20
$$\begin{array}{r} 307 \\ -\ 295 \\ \hline \end{array}$$

21
$$\begin{array}{r} 492 \\ -\ 374 \\ \hline \end{array}$$

22
$$\begin{array}{r} 770 \\ +\ 199 \\ \hline \end{array}$$

23
$$\begin{array}{r} 700 \\ -\ 201 \\ \hline \end{array}$$

Answer the following questions.

24 On school days, Jun needs at least 20 minutes to eat breakfast, 3 minutes to brush his teeth, 15 minutes to get dressed, and 7 minutes to gather all the materials he needs. What's the least amount of time it takes Jun to get ready for school?

25 At the beginning of the school year Park Elementary had 311 students. During the year, 14 students moved away and 12 new students entered the school. How many students were there at the end of the school year?

26 **Extended Response** In 1990 the population of Park City was about 4,468. In 2000 the population was about 7,371. By about how much did the population increase?

Explain how you could estimate to find an answer for this problem.

27 Damon and his friends went bowling. In his first game Damon had a score of 131. Halfway through his second game he had a score of 89. How many more points did he need in the second game to beat his previous score?

28 Ronda wants to use her babysitting money to pay for a new bicycle. She kept track of the money she earned for 4 weeks. She earned $15 the first week, $25 the second week, $20 the third week, and $27 the fourth week. How much more money does she need to make in order to buy a bicycle that costs $120?

SOCIAL STUDIES **29** John F. Kennedy was born on May 29, 1917. He became president on January 20, 1961. How old was he when he became president?

30 Ronald Reagan was born on February 6, 1911. He became president on January 20, 1981. How old was he when he became president?

e Textbook This lesson is available in the *eTextbook*.

Game

Roll a Problem Game

Players: Two or more

Materials: *Number Cube:* One 0–5 (red)

Object: To get the smallest difference greater than or equal to 0

Math Focus: Multidigit arithmetic, place value, and mathematical reasoning

HOW TO PLAY

1 Use blanks to outline a subtraction problem on your paper, like this:

____ ____ ____
– ____ ____ ____
‾‾‾‾‾‾‾‾‾‾‾‾‾‾

2 The first player rolls the *Number Cube* six times.

3 After each time the cube is rolled, each player writes that number in one of the blanks in his or her outline. Then the cube is rolled again. A zero may be put in any place, including the first.

4 When all the blanks have been filled in, each player finds the difference of the three-digit numbers they created.

5 The player with the least difference greater than or equal to 0 is the winner.

Other Ways to Play This Game

- Try to get the greatest difference.

- Change the number of digits.

- Add. Decide in advance whether the winner will have the greatest or least sum.

- Use the 5–10 *Number Cube,* and reroll if a 10 appears.

 **Journal**

Which exercise on page 53 did you find easiest because of a shortcut you used? Explain the shortcut.

Multidigit Addition and Subtraction

Key Ideas

Addition and subtraction can be used to solve many problems involving large numbers.

Add or subtract.

1 $\begin{array}{r} 70 \\ -\ 40 \\ \hline \end{array}$	**2** $\begin{array}{r} 70 \\ -\ 39 \\ \hline \end{array}$	**3** $\begin{array}{r} 70 \\ -\ 38 \\ \hline \end{array}$	**4** $\begin{array}{r} 71 \\ -\ 38 \\ \hline \end{array}$	**5** $\begin{array}{r} 38 \\ +\ 50 \\ \hline \end{array}$
6 $\begin{array}{r} 38 \\ +\ 49 \\ \hline \end{array}$	**7** $\begin{array}{r} 38 \\ +\ 48 \\ \hline \end{array}$	**8** $\begin{array}{r} 354 \\ +\ 645 \\ \hline \end{array}$	**9** $\begin{array}{r} 354 \\ +\ 646 \\ \hline \end{array}$	**10** $\begin{array}{r} 999 \\ -\ 873 \\ \hline \end{array}$
11 $\begin{array}{r} 1000 \\ -\ 873 \\ \hline \end{array}$	**12** $\begin{array}{r} 83 \\ +\ 28 \\ \hline \end{array}$	**13** $\begin{array}{r} 368 \\ +\ 121 \\ \hline \end{array}$	**14** $\begin{array}{r} 529 \\ +\ 310 \\ \hline \end{array}$	**15** $\begin{array}{r} 476 \\ -\ 287 \\ \hline \end{array}$
16 $\begin{array}{r} 687 \\ -\ 321 \\ \hline \end{array}$	**17** $\begin{array}{r} 568 \\ -\ 37 \\ \hline \end{array}$	**18** $\begin{array}{r} 329 \\ +\ 692 \\ \hline \end{array}$	**19** $\begin{array}{r} 474 \\ +\ 289 \\ \hline \end{array}$	**20** $\begin{array}{r} 274 \\ +\ 189 \\ \hline \end{array}$
21 $\begin{array}{r} 6725 \\ +\ 1235 \\ \hline \end{array}$	**22** $\begin{array}{r} 7925 \\ +\ 2136 \\ \hline \end{array}$	**23** $\begin{array}{r} 2748 \\ -\ 1692 \\ \hline \end{array}$	**24** $\begin{array}{r} 1897 \\ -\ 769 \\ \hline \end{array}$	**25** $\begin{array}{r} 28133 \\ -\ 14960 \\ \hline \end{array}$

26 Clara and Tomás ran for school president. Clara got 743 votes. Tomás got 916 votes.

   a. Who won?

   b. By how many votes?

   c. How many students attend the school?

   d. How many people voted?

ⓔ Textbook This lesson is available in the *eTextbook.*

Planet	Average Distance from Sun (in millions of miles)	Diameter (in miles)
Mercury	37	3,032
Venus	65	7,522
Earth	93	7,920
Mars	140	4,214
Jupiter	484	86,900
Saturn	884	72,382
Uranus	1,796	31,524
Neptune	2,790	30,608
Pluto	3,627	1,486

Diameter is the length of a straight line segment passing through the center of a circle or sphere from one side to the other.

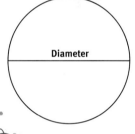

Diameter

Answer the following questions based on the table.

27 How much greater is the diameter of Earth than the diameter of Mars?

28 What is the difference between the average distances from the sun to Neptune and to Earth?

29 Jupiter's greatest distance from the sun is about 24 million miles greater than its average distance. About how far is Jupiter's greatest distance from the sun?

30 Which two planets have the least difference in diameter? What is the difference between their diameters?

31 Which two planets have the greatest difference in diameter? What is the difference between their diameters?

32 Suppose Earth and Venus are both at their average distances from the sun. What is the closest they could be to each other? What is the farthest they could be from each other?

Answer these questions.

Amalia needs 55¢ to mail an oversized greeting card. She has these stamps:

33 Can Amalia make exactly 55¢ in postage stamps?

34 Which stamps make exactly 55¢?

35 How many postage stamps will Amalia have left?

36 What will be the total value of the stamps she has left?

Three children are collecting baseball cards.
Lia has 742 cards, Peter has 643, and A. J. has 392.

37 How many more cards does A. J. need to have as many as Lia?

38 How many more cards does Peter need to have as many as Lia?

39 Suppose Peter gives A. J. 343 cards. Will A. J. then have as many cards as Lia?

40 Suppose Lia gives A. J. 200 cards. Will A. J. then have just as many cards as Lia?

41 **Extended Response** How many cards would Lia have to give to A. J. for them to have the same number? Explain how you found your answer.

e Textbook This lesson is available in the *eTextbook.*

Sasha made a chart to help her find the least expensive supermarket. The first thing she decided was which items she wanted.

Complete the bottom row of Sasha's chart.

Item	Price		
	So-Low Supermarket	Hi-Value Supermarket	Bargain Town Supermarket
1 dozen eggs (large Grade AA)	$1.09	$1.05	$1.15
1 quart of apple juice (Top-Core brand)	$1.25	$1.37	$1.29
2 pounds of potatoes	$0.88	$0.96	$0.80
Total	▪	▪	▪

Use the chart to answer these questions.

42 Which supermarket is least expensive for the three items listed?

43 Which supermarket is most expensive?

44 If Sasha paid for the three items at the So-Low Supermarket with a $5 bill, how much change would she get?

45 **Extended Response** Sasha met Mr. Tanaka, who was going shopping. "I have to buy bread, butter, apples, and peanut butter," said Mr. Tanaka. "Do you know which supermarket will be the least expensive?" he asked. Does Sasha know the answer to Mr. Tanaka's question? Why or why not?

Writing + Math **Journal**

How would you decide which of two stores has better prices? If you and another person each made a grocery list and compared the prices at two stores, do you think the two of you might reach different conclusions.

Using Relation Signs

Key Ideas

Inequality signs are used to show which of two numbers is greater. The open end of an inequality sign points towards the greater number, and the pointed end points towards the smaller number. Equal signs are used to show that two values are the same.

What do these signs mean? $<$ $>$ $=$

Look at these examples:

$25 < 30$ means
25 **is less than** 30.

$10 > 7 + 1$ means
10 **is greater than** $7 + 1$.

$4 + 9 = 8 + 5$ means
$4 + 9$ **is equal to** $8 + 5$.

Copy each exercise and insert $<$, $>$, or $=$ to make a true statement. **Algebra**

1. $27 \;\rule{1em}{0.8em}\; 19$
2. $11 \;\rule{1em}{0.8em}\; 77 + 66$
3. $39 \;\rule{1em}{0.8em}\; 52 + 49$

4. $36 \;\rule{1em}{0.8em}\; 18$
5. $79 \;\rule{1em}{0.8em}\; 77 + 10$
6. $8 + 9 \;\rule{1em}{0.8em}\; 8 - 2$

7. $19 \;\rule{1em}{0.8em}\; 79$
8. $16 \;\rule{1em}{0.8em}\; 21 + 3$
9. $18 - 9 \;\rule{1em}{0.8em}\; 18 + 3$

10. $4 + 3 \;\rule{1em}{0.8em}\; 3 + 4$
11. $56 \;\rule{1em}{0.8em}\; 40 + 20$
12. $33 - 6 \;\rule{1em}{0.8em}\; 33 - 7$

13. $9 \;\rule{1em}{0.8em}\; 19 + 10$
14. $39 \;\rule{1em}{0.8em}\; 29 + 29$
15. $49 + 3 \;\rule{1em}{0.8em}\; 49 + 5$

16. $100 \;\rule{1em}{0.8em}\; 73 + 10$
17. $63 \;\rule{1em}{0.8em}\; 33 + 23$
18. $77 - 16 \;\rule{1em}{0.8em}\; 74 - 16$

19. $84 \;\rule{1em}{0.8em}\; 73 - 10$
20. $55 \;\rule{1em}{0.8em}\; 55 - 13$
21. $20 - 15 \;\rule{1em}{0.8em}\; 25 - 10$

22. Mr. Bannerji has $100. Does he have enough money to pay for

    a. a jacket and a tie?

    b. a pair of pants and a sweater?

    c. a sweater and 3 ties?

Textbook This lesson is available in the *eTextbook*.

Game

Inequalities and Strategies Practice

Inequality Game

Players: Two

Materials: *Number Cubes:* two 0–5 (red), two 5–10 (blue)

Object: To fill in an inequality statement correctly

Math Focus: Identifying inequalities, mathematical reasoning

HOW TO PLAY

① Make one of these game forms on a sheet of paper

$$\underline{\quad\quad} < \underline{\quad\quad} \quad \text{or} \quad \underline{\quad\quad} > \underline{\quad\quad}$$

② Player 1 rolls all four **Number Cubes**, makes two two-digit numbers, and writes their sum on either side of the inequality sign. If a cube lands on 10, roll that cube again. A zero may be placed in the tens place. So, for example, 08 is acceptable.

③ Player 2 rolls all four cubes, makes two two-digit numbers, and writes his or her sum in the remaining space.

④ If the inequality statement is true, Player 2 wins. If the inequality statement is false, Player 1 wins.

⑤ Players take turns being first.

Other Ways to Play This Game

● Find the difference between the two two-digit numbers.

● Each player gets to choose whether to add or subtract.

 **Journal**

If you were playing the **Inequality Game** and could choose which number to roll, which numbers would you choose? If you could choose not to have a certain number appear when you roll the cubes, which number would you choose?

Exploring Problem Solving

Ed collects cards and trades them with his friends. Last Tuesday he began to keep track of his trades.

Day	Traded with	Number of Cards I Gave	Number of Cards I Got
Tuesday	Roberta	14	12
Wednesday	Andreas	8	13
Friday	Yoshiko	17	11
Saturday	Bought 10 cards	0	10
Saturday	David	5	9

After he traded with David, Ed had 129 cards. Ed remembers that he counted his cards Monday morning before he started keeping records. He had 131 cards. Then he traded with Amelia on Monday afternoon. He wonders how many cards he traded with Amelia.

Ed solved the problem this way:

I started by Working Backward.

I had 129 cards after the trade with David.
Before I got 9 cards from David, I had 120. $129 - 9 = 120$
Before I gave 5 cards to David, I had 125. $120 + 5 = 125$
So, I had 125 cards before trading with David.

Think about Ed's strategy. Answer these questions.

1. Why did Ed subtract to find out how many cards he had before he got 9 from David?

2. Why did Ed add to find out how many cards he had before he gave 5 to David?

3. How many cards did Ed have before Saturday?

e Textbook This lesson is available in the *eTextbook*.

Ed decided to try a different strategy.

I Made a Table to show more information.

Day	Traded with	Number of Cards I Gave	Number of Cards I Got	What I Gained or Lost
Monday	Amelia	?	?	?
Tuesday	Roberta	14	12	lost 2
Wednesday	Andreas	8	13	gained 5
Friday	Yoshiko	17	11	lost 6
Saturday	Bought 10 cards	0	10	gained 10
Saturday	David	5	9	gained 4

End Result: gained 19, lost 8

Think about Ed's second strategy. Answer these questions.

4. What does Ed's new table have that his original table did not?

5. Did Ed have more or fewer cards on Saturday than he had on Tuesday? How do you know?

6. How many fewer cards did Ed have on Tuesday than on Saturday? Explain.

7. Do you think Ed's second strategy will solve the problem? Explain.

8. Which of Ed's two strategies do you prefer? Why? Use one of Ed's strategies or a strategy of your own to solve the problem.

Cumulative Review

Study the chart below. Then answer the questions.

Telephone Lines			
Country	Main Lines	Cellular Phones	Percentage of People Who Use Cellular
United States	178,000,000	55,312,000	23%
Mexico	9,600,000	2,020,000	17%
Canada	18,500,000	3,000,000	13%
France	34,860,000	11,078,000	24%
Ireland	1,642,541	941,775	36%
China	110,000,000	23,400,000	17%
Japan	60,300,000	36,500,000	37%

1. Which country listed on the chart above has the highest number of main lines?

2. How many cell phone lines does Ireland have?

3. Which country has the highest percentage of cell phone lines? How many do they have?

4. In which country do only 13% of the people use cell phone lines?

5. What is the difference in the number of main phone lines between China and the United States?

Place Value Lesson 1.2

Name the place that 9 is in for each number below.

6. 79,634

7. 23,459

8. 3,490,176

9. $392.56

10. 98

Missing Addends Lesson 1.7

Solve for *n*.

⑪ $n + 4 = 9$ ⑫ $7 - n = 2$ ⑬ $18 + n = 25$

⑭ Clem owns 7 horses. He needs 12 horses to open a riding stable. How many more horses does he need?

⑮ Daria had $9. Then she did chores and earned $8. Does she have enough money to buy a CD that costs $14?

- -

Perimeter Lesson 1.8

Find the perimeter.

⑯
12 mm

3 mm

⑰
4 ft

4 ft

⑱ A rectangle has a perimeter of 24 feet. Which of the following could be the lengths of the sides of the rectangle?

Ⓐ 4 ft and 8 ft   Ⓑ 6 ft and 4 ft

Ⓒ 12 ft and 2 ft   Ⓓ 8 ft and 3 ft

⑲ A square with a side length of 7 feet has a perimeter of

Ⓐ 14 ft   Ⓑ 7 ft

Ⓒ 28 ft   Ⓓ 21 ft

⑳ The length of one side of a rectangle is 15. What could its perimeter be?

Ⓐ 18   Ⓑ 30

Ⓒ 25   Ⓓ 40

Addition and Subtraction with Hidden Digits

Key Ideas

Using what you already know about numbers, you can solve problems containing missing digits.

Paint was spilled on these two pages. One answer is correct in each case. Decide which answer is correct.

What are some methods that could be used for solving these problems?

Example: 23
              + 4🔵

    a. 51

    b. 61

    c. 71

The sum must be at least 63. It could be as much as 72. The correct answer must be 71.

Select the appropriate answer using what you know about addition and subtraction.

1   68
   + 2🔵

    a. 86

    b. 96

    c. 106

2   204
   + 7🔵

    a. 99

    b. 279

    c. 949

3   53🔵
   + 330

    a. 259

    b. 863

    c. 1,059

4   2🔵5
   + 3🔵

    a. 83

    b. 492

    c. 613

5   456
   + 31🔵

    a. 143

    b. 769

    c. 283

6   670🔵
   + 🔵

    a. 4,159

    b. 6,532

    c. 9,705

7   87
   − 3🔵

    a. 51

    b. 64

    c. 92

8   82
   − 3🔵

    a. 46

    b. 56

    c. 66

🔲**Textbook** This lesson is available in the *eTextbook*.

Use whatever procedures you wish to solve the following:

1 $5 - (-5) =$ ▢

2 $5 + (+5) =$ ▢

3 $5 - (-3) =$ ▢

4 $-18 - (-2) =$ ▢

5 $5 - (+5) =$ ▢

6 $8 + (-3) =$ ▢

7 $8 - (+3) =$ ▢

8 $-7 + (-8) =$ ▢

Note: We often write parentheses around some of the numbers to avoid confusing the positive and negative signs with the signs for addition and subtraction.

Also, notice that we often do not write parentheses around positive numbers, and usually do not write the "+" symbol in front of them.

9 $-12 + 5 =$ ▢

10 $-12 - 5 =$ ▢

11 $12 + 5 =$ ▢

12 $12 - 5 =$ ▢

13 $-3 - (-5) =$ ▢

14 $0 - (-3) =$ ▢

15 $0 + (-3) =$ ▢

16 $2 - (-3) =$ ▢

17 $5 - 8 =$ ▢

18 $5 + (-5) =$ ▢

19 $8 - (-3) =$ ▢

20 $24 - (-7) =$ ▢

Solve the following problems.

21 The bank tells you that the balance in your checking account is $37. You believe the balance should be more, and ask the bank to check their records. It turns out that they have charged $81 to your account that they should not have charged. When they take away that $81 charge, what will your balance be?

22 A deep sea diver is 23 feet below sea level. She swims down another 10 feet. How far below sea level is she now?

23 The weather reporter announces that the temperature is now 3° but he expects it to go down 17° by this time tomorrow. What is he predicting the temperature will be?

SCIENCE

24 The weather reporter later says he made a mistake. He now believes the temperature will go up 17°. In this case, what will the temperature be?

25 I know the temperature is now −4°, and it has gone down 9° since last night at 6:00 P.M. What was the temperature at 6:00 P.M. yesterday?

June 18

Playground by Kids, For Kids

New York City

What was unusual about elementary school students gathering today at the new playground in the Mott Haven section of the Bronx? The students were dedicating the playground that they had designed.

Kids from PS 43 used to spend their recess on a section of the street marked off by orange traffic cones. Thanks to many generous supporters and to the hard work of the student planners, these children and the rest of the community now have a better and safer place to play.

The block-wide facility, called Ranaqua Park, contains a basketball court, a grass field, swings, and other play equipment.

The $400,000 recreational space is one of many parks and playgrounds built as part of the City Spaces program of the Trust for Public Land.

use zone

Field of Dreams

When they designed Ranaqua Park, the students at PS 43 had to pay close attention to safety regulations. For example, they had to make sure there was enough space and protective surfacing for each piece of equipment.

The **use zone** is an area under and around the equipment where protective surfacing is required. The use zone should be free of obstacles that children could run into or fall on top of.

Ⓔ Textbook This lesson is available in the *eTextbook*.

Safety Regulations

Because children may deliberately attempt to exit from a swing while it is in motion, the use zone in front of and behind the swing should be greater than to the sides.

The use zone should extend to the front and rear of a swing a minimum distance of twice the height of the pivot point above the surfacing material. The use zone to the sides of a swing should extend a minimum of 6 feet from the perimeter of the swing structure.

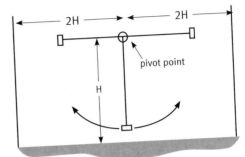

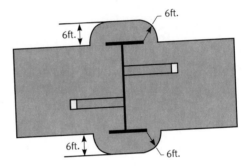

Adapted from *Handbook for Public Playground Safety*
U.S. Consumer Product Safety Commission

Solve these problems. Use the information on both pages to help you.

1. Why does the use zone go beyond where the swing can reach?

2. If the pivot point of a swing is 10 feet above the ground, how long must the use zone be?

3. If a swing set is 10 feet wide, how wide must the use zone be?

Exploring Problem Solving

Imagine the students at your school, like the students at PS 43, are designing a playground. Your group is in charge of designing a swing set that will fit within the rectangular use zone that is 45 feet long and 28 feet wide. You want to include as many swings on the swing set as you can. But the swing set must meet all the safety requirements described below and on pages 76–77.

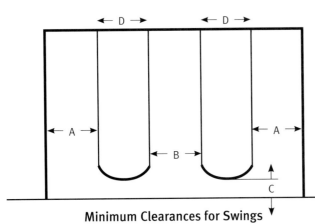

Minimum Clearances for Swings

A: minimum 30 in.

B: minimum 24 in.

C: minimum 16 in.

D: minimum 20 in.

Solve these problems. Show your work.

4 Draw a diagram to show your design for the swing set. Label all the important lengths. Also draw and label a diagram of the use zone.

5 Copy and complete this chart to describe your swing set.

Number of Swings	Height of Swing Set (H)	Distance Between Swings (B)	Distance Between Swing and Support (A)	Width of Swings (D)	Length of Use Zone	Width of Use Zone (D)
▪	▪	▪	▪	▪	▪	▪

6 What strategies did you use to design your swing set?

Cumulative Review

Practicing Addition and Subtraction Lesson 1.5

Add or subtract to solve for *n*.

1 $7 + 6 = n$

2 $4 + 9 = n$

3 $14 - 9 = n$

4 $17 - 8 = n$

5 $13 - 8 = n$

Function Machines Lesson 1.6

Complete each chart. Watch the function rule.

6
in -7 out	
19	
16	
14	
11	

7
in $+10$ out	
0	
3	
8	
10	

8
in $+5$ out	
20	
30	
40	
50	

9
in -2 out	
100	
96	
92	
90	

Cumulative Review

Place Value Lesson 1.2

Write the numbers in standard form.

⑩ 50 + 9

⑪ 8 + 30

⑫ 500 + 30 + 7

⑬ 4,000 + 200 + 40 + 0

⑭ 40,000 + 500 + 70 + 2

⑮ 3 + 400 + 40,000 + 100,000

⑯ 300,000 + 4,000 + 70

⑰ 2,000,000 + 40,000 + 6,000 + 800 + 10

⑱ 500,000 + 200

⑲ 3 + 80 + 200 + 40,000 + 90,000,000

Numerical Sequence Lesson 1.3

Count up or down. Write the missing numbers.

⑳ 15, 16, 17, ▢, ▢, ▢, ▢, ▢, 23

㉑ 97, 98, 99, ▢, ▢, ▢, ▢, 104

㉒ 403, 402, 401, ▢, ▢, ▢, ▢, ▢, 395

㉓ 45,677; 45,678; 45,679; ▢; ▢; ▢; ▢; 45,684

㉔ 1,000,204; 1,000,203; 1,000,202 ▢; ▢; ▢; ▢; 1,000,197

Rounding Lesson 1.4

Round each number to the nearest ten.

㉕ 684

㉖ 957

㉗ 4,289

Round each number to the nearest hundred.

㉘ 957

㉙ 1,567

㉚ 98,231

Round each number to the nearest thousand.

㉛ 3,099

㉜ 16,487

㉝ 554,623

㉞ 34,604

ⓔ Textbook This lesson is available in the *eTextbook*.

Key Ideas Review

In this chapter you learned strategies to add and subtract multidigit numbers.

You learned how to regroup when subtracting greater numbers.

You learned how to compare numbers and use numerical values to approximate and infer answers.

Select an answer from the box and match it with an exercise.

| 4,378 | 192 | 142 | 4,296 |

1
$$1793$$
$$+\ 2503$$

2
$$1003$$
$$-\ 861$$

3
$$902$$
$$-\ 710$$

Select the appropriate relation sign.

4 45 + 32 ■ 98 − 22

    a. < **b.** > **c.** =

5 31 ■ 57 − 26

    a. < **b.** > **c.** =

6 100 + 20 ■ 200 + 10

    a. < **b.** > **c.** =

Decide whether or not each problem has enough information to solve it.

7 Alekya is planning a trip from Raleigh, North Carolina, to St. Louis, Missouri. She has a stop in Chicago, Illinois, which is 641 miles from Raleigh. How many more miles does she need to go to get to St. Louis?

8 Pierre runs about 2 miles every day while playing soccer. If the school year is 182 days long, about how many miles will he run during the school year? Explain how you approximated your answer.

Chapter Review

Lesson 2.1 **Find** the sum.

①	56	②	83	③	186	④	39	⑤	346
	+ 97		+ 46		+ 39		+ 208		+ 287

Lesson 2.2 **Find** the difference.

⑥	793	⑦	92	⑧	607	⑨	573	⑩	491
	− 200		− 67		− 289		− 381		− 268

Lesson 2.3 **Add** or subtract. Watch the signs.

⑪	593	⑫	43572	⑬	53408761	⑭	61204
	+ 248		− 1281		+ 721508		− 34561

Lesson 2.4 **Replace** ▒ in each statement with >, <, or =.

⑮ 25 + 20 ▒ 30 + 15   ⑰ 13 − 10 ▒ 22 − 15

⑯ 18 − 9 ▒ 16 − 7   ⑱ 6 + 5 ▒ 14 − 5

Lesson 2.5 **Find** the missing digit.

⑲	407	⑳	602	㉑	321	㉒	775	㉓	274
	− 229		− 345		− 285		− 391		− 106
	1 ▒ 8		25 ▒		▒ 6		3 ▒ 4		16 ▒

e Textbook This lesson is available in the *eTextbook*.

Lesson 2.6

24 **Extended Response** There are 137 students taking buses to visit a toy factory. Each bus holds 30 students.

  a. Will 4 buses be too few, just enough, or too many to hold all the students? Explain your answer.

  b. How many buses are needed?

  c. If it costs $60 to rent 1 bus, how much will it cost to rent all the buses for the trip?

Lesson 2.7

25 **Extended Response** Lisa earns money for babysitting after school. The following was her schedule last week:

Day	Earnings
Monday	$10
Tuesday	$8
Wednesday	$12
Thursday	$15
Friday	$5

Lisa usually gets paid on the same day that she works, but last week there were two days on which she worked but did not get paid. If she has already received $37 for last week's work, then for which two days did she not receive pay? Explain.

Lessons 2.8 and 2.9

Solve.

26 $-12 + 5$

  a. -6

  b. 7

  c. -7

27 $-8 - (-2)$

  a. 6

  b. -6

  c. -10

28 $-3 + (-5)$

  a. -8

  b. 8

  c. -2

Find the sum.

Find the difference.

1. 470
   + 208

   Ⓐ 478   Ⓑ 688

   Ⓒ 678   Ⓓ 488

6. 60
   − 37

   Ⓐ 33   Ⓑ 23

   Ⓒ 13   Ⓓ 27

2. 3408
   + 2697

   Ⓐ 6105   Ⓑ 6015

   Ⓒ 6005   Ⓓ 5105

7. 589
   − 280

   Ⓐ 309   Ⓑ 319

   Ⓒ 299   Ⓓ 399

3. 210
   + 25

   Ⓐ 225   Ⓑ 215

   Ⓒ 235   Ⓓ 335

8. 260
   − 173

   Ⓐ 77   Ⓑ 87

   Ⓒ 97   Ⓓ 83

4. 789
   + 300

   Ⓐ 1189   Ⓑ 1089

   Ⓒ 1099   Ⓓ 792

9. 3508
   − 809

   Ⓐ 2799   Ⓑ 2701

   Ⓒ 2699   Ⓓ 2601

5. 3461
   + 2879

   Ⓐ 6240   Ⓑ 6230

   Ⓒ 6300   Ⓓ 6340

10. 6379
    − 370

    Ⓐ 6009   Ⓑ 5909

    Ⓒ 5919   Ⓓ 6749

ⓔ Textbook This lesson is available in the *eTextbook*.

Add or subtract. Watch the signs.

11. 145
       − 88

Ⓐ 67   Ⓑ 75

Ⓒ 57   Ⓓ 66

12. 765
       + 567

Ⓐ 1,232   Ⓑ 1,332

Ⓒ 1,222   Ⓓ 1,422

13. 6379
       − 370

Ⓐ 6,009   Ⓑ 5,909

Ⓒ 5,919   Ⓓ 6,749

14. 804,721
       − 712,438

Ⓐ 92,283   Ⓑ 91,283

Ⓒ 90,293   Ⓓ 91,383

15. 666
       + 382

Ⓐ 1,048   Ⓑ 948

Ⓒ 1,064   Ⓓ 1,148

Write the correct symbol for each statement.

16. $5 + 7 \; \blacksquare \; 3 + 8$

Ⓐ $>$

Ⓑ $<$

Ⓒ $=$

17. $13 - 6 \; \blacksquare \; 16 - 7$

Ⓐ $>$

Ⓑ $<$

Ⓒ $=$

18. $12 + 9 \; \blacksquare \; 11 + 6$

Ⓐ $>$

Ⓑ $<$

Ⓒ $=$

19. $13 - 10 \; \blacksquare \; 22 - 15$

Ⓐ $>$

Ⓑ $<$

Ⓒ $=$

20. $6 + 3 \; \blacksquare \; 14 - 5$

Ⓐ $>$

Ⓑ $<$

Ⓒ $=$

Find the missing digit to determine the correct answer.

21.
```
   4 7
 + 2 ▓
 ─────
   7 6
```

Ⓐ 9   Ⓑ 3

Ⓒ 8   Ⓓ 5

22.
```
   6 0 2
 - 3 ▓ ▓
 ───────
   2 3 7
```

Ⓐ 47   Ⓑ 56

Ⓒ 67   Ⓓ 65

23.
```
   3 2 1
 + 2 ▓ 5
 ───────
   5 4 6
```

Ⓐ 3   Ⓑ 1

Ⓒ 2   Ⓓ 5

24.
```
   7 8 5
 - 3 ▓ 1
 ───────
   3 9 4
```

Ⓐ 8   Ⓑ 9

Ⓒ 6   Ⓓ 4

25.
```
   ▓ 7 4
 + 1 0 6
 ───────
   4 8 0
```

Ⓐ 3   Ⓑ 8

Ⓒ 6   Ⓓ 4

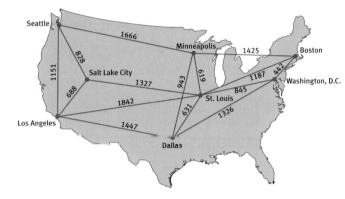

Approximate your answers using the map above.

26. About how many miles is it from Los Angeles to Dallas to St. Louis?

Ⓐ 1,500   Ⓑ 2,000

Ⓒ 2,500   Ⓓ 3,000

27. About how many more miles is it from Seattle to Minneapolis than it is from Seattle to Los Angeles?

Ⓐ 100   Ⓑ 300

Ⓒ 500   Ⓓ 700

28. About how much farther is it from Los Angeles to Dallas than from Minneapolis to Boston?

Ⓐ about the same   Ⓑ 500

Ⓒ 750   Ⓓ 1,000

29. About how much farther is it to go from Minneapolis to Boston with a stop in St. Louis than it is to go without stopping?

Ⓐ 200 miles   Ⓑ 400 miles

Ⓒ 600 miles   Ⓓ 800 miles

ⓔ **Textbook** This lesson is available in the *eTextbook*.

Extended Response ➤ **Solve** the following exercises.

The store manager made a chart of the number of shirts sold in a week. The bottom was ruined when he spilled coffee on it. Study what is left.

Day	Number of Shirts Sold
Monday	35
Tuesday	25
Wednesday	37
Thursday	29
Friday	29
Saturday	

30. The manager began the week with 200 shirts in stock. Do you think he will have enough to sell on Saturday and Sunday? Explain why or why not.

31. If the store is closed on Sunday, will he have enough on Saturday? Explain.

32. Charlie is washing cars to earn money to buy a scooter. The scooter costs $80. He washed 5 cars this week. His earnings per day were $8, $12, $15, $18, and $20. Did Charlie earn enough this week to purchase the scooter? Explain.

33. Charlie's friend Peggy said, "Charlie, if you had charged $2 more per car, you could have had enough money to buy the scooter." Is Peggy correct?

34. Other than adding, is there a quicker way to figure out how much more money Charlie would have if he had charged $2 more per car? Explain.

Multiplication and Division

In This Chapter You Will Learn

- strategies for finding multiplication facts through 12×12.
- how to use different laws of multiplication.
- strategies for division with remainders.

Problem Solving

Imagine that you are working for a company that is making a new portable music player. Your task is to decide what size shipping carton to order for the player.

Shipping Information

Each SongBird music player comes in its own box.

The shipping carton must hold 48 music players.

The carton should be as small and easy to handle as possible.

Work in groups. Answer these questions.

1. What size shipping carton will you order? Give the length, height, and width.

2. Describe how the 48 music players will fit in the carton.

3. How did you solve this problem?

4. What additions would you make to the shipping carton so it would be easier to carry?

Understanding Multiplication

Key Ideas

You can do multiplication in different ways.

For example, to find the answer to 4×3, you can:

use the lattice method. Draw 4 vertical lines and draw 3 horizontal lines that intersect, or go through, the vertical lines. Count the number of places where the lines intersect.

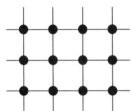

$$3 \times 4 = 12$$

use skip counting. To find 3×4, you can skip count by 4s to 12.

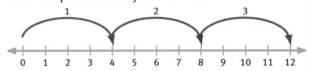

Think of multiplication as repeated addition. To find 4×3, you can add 4 three times.

$$4 + 4 + 4 = 12$$

Use one of the methods above to calculate the following. **Algebra**

1. $7 \times 6 = n$
2. $6 \times 7 = n$
3. $7 \times 7 = n$
4. $9 \times 8 = n$
5. $8 \times 8 = n$
6. $2 \times 2 = n$
7. $3 \times 4 = n$
8. $5 \times 0 = n$
9. $7 \times 8 = n$
10. $0 \times 5 = n$
11. $8 \times 7 = n$
12. $10 \times 10 = n$
13. $1 \times 7 = n$
14. $8 \times 8 = n$
15. $11 \times 12 = n$

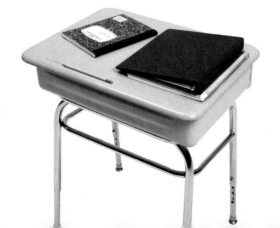

e Textbook This lesson is available in the *eTextbook.*

You have learned that the order in which you add two numbers does not affect their sum. For example:

$$283 + 971 = 1254 \quad \text{and} \quad 971 + 283 = 1254$$

You also can multiply numbers in any order. The order in which two numbers are multiplied does not affect their **product.**

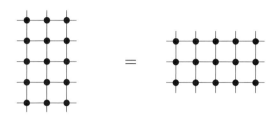

$$3 \times 5 = 15 \quad \text{and} \quad 5 \times 3 = 15$$

You can add numbers in any order to get the same sum. This is called the Commutative Law for addition. Likewise, you can multiply numbers in any order and get the same product. This is called the Commutative Law for Multiplication.

Solve for *n*.

16 $2 \times 5 = n$
$5 \times 2 = n$

17 $9 \times 0 = n$
$0 \times 9 = n$

18 $6 \times 9 = n$
$9 \times 6 = n$

19 $1 \times 8 = n$
$8 \times 1 = n$

20 $3 \times 4 = n$
$4 \times 3 = n$

21 $7 \times 9 = n$
$9 \times 7 = n$

22 $10 \times 4 = n$
$4 \times 10 = n$

23 $3 \times 9 = n$
$9 \times 3 = n$

24 $6 \times 4 = n$
$4 \times 6 = n$

25 $5 \times 8 = n$
$8 \times 5 = n$

26 $4 \times 8 = n$
$8 \times 4 = n$

27 $7 \times 8 = n$
$8 \times 7 = n$

28 **Extended Response** Mrs. Weiss needs to find a room with desks for each of her 28 students. In room 211, there are 6 rows of 5 desks. Are there enough desks? Explain.

29 **Extended Response** If the desks in room 211 were arranged in 5 rows of 6 desks would there still be enough desks for all 28 students? Explain.

30 Sheila buys 2 necklaces and 3 bracelets as gifts for her friends. Each item cost $6. How much money did Sheila spend altogether?

Multiplying by 0, 1, 2, and 10

Key Ideas

There are quick and simple ways to multiply numbers by 0, 1, 2, and 10.

Multiplying a number by 2 is the same as doubling it or adding it to itself.

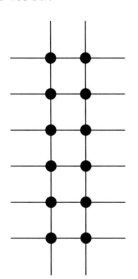

$2 \times 6 = 12$
or $6 + 6 = 12$

Multiplying a number by 1 simply means taking 1 of that number.

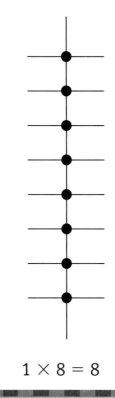

$1 \times 8 = 8$

Multiplying a number by 0 means taking none of that number.

$0 \times 7 = 0$

Multiples of 10 are written with a 0 after the multiple. For example, 4 tens is 40.

$10 \times 4 = 40$

Answer the following questions.

There are 7 days in a week.

1. How many days are in 2 weeks?

2. How many days are in 1 week?

3. How many days are in 3 weeks?

4. How many days are in 10 weeks?

Multiply to solve for *n*. **Algebra**

5. $0 \times 5 = n$

6. $10 \times 2 = n$

7. $4 \times 10 = n$

8. $8 \times 1 = n$

9. $6 \times 2 = n$

10. $9 \times 2 = n$

11. $5 \times 0 = n$

12. $1 \times 9 = n$

13. $2 \times 9 = n$

14. $1 \times 8 = n$

Find each product.

15.
$$\begin{array}{r} 6 \\ \times\ 2 \\ \hline \end{array}$$

16.
$$\begin{array}{r} 7 \\ \times\ 10 \\ \hline \end{array}$$

17.
$$\begin{array}{r} 10 \\ \times\ 8 \\ \hline \end{array}$$

18.
$$\begin{array}{r} 8 \\ \times\ 10 \\ \hline \end{array}$$

19.
$$\begin{array}{r} 4 \\ \times\ 10 \\ \hline \end{array}$$

20.
$$\begin{array}{r} 10 \\ \times\ 2 \\ \hline \end{array}$$

21.
$$\begin{array}{r} 8 \\ \times\ 0 \\ \hline \end{array}$$

22.
$$\begin{array}{r} 5 \\ \times\ 2 \\ \hline \end{array}$$

23.
$$\begin{array}{r} 8 \\ \times\ 7 \\ \hline \end{array}$$

24.
$$\begin{array}{r} 7 \\ \times\ 8 \\ \hline \end{array}$$

25. Ted went to a sports card show with 6 cards to trade. When he left the show **SOCIAL STUDIES** he had 10 times the number of cards he started with. How many cards did Ted have?

26. Ted's sister Vanessa went to the show too. She had 5 baseball cards and 2 basketball cards to sell. Someone offered her $2 for each card. If she accepts the offer, how much money will she make?

27. **Extended Response** Is it possible to multiply a whole number by 10 and get a product of 63? Explain how you know.

Writing + Math **Journal**

Explain the strategy you use to remember the multiplication facts for larger numbers.

Multiplying by 5 and by 9

Key Ideas

You can use what you know about multiplying by 10 to help you multiply by 5 and 9.

✕	0	1	2	3	4	5	6	7	8	9	10
0	0	0	0	0	0	0	0	0	0	0	0
1	0	1	2	3	4	5	6	7	8	9	10
2	0	2	4	6	8	10	12	14	16	18	20
3	0	3	6	9	12	15	18	21	24	27	30
4	0	4	8	12	16	20	24	28	32	36	40
5	0	5	10	15	20	25	30	35	40	45	50
6	0	6	12	18	24	30	36	42	48	54	60
7	0	7	14	21	28	35	42	49	56	63	70
8	0	8	16	24	32	40	48	56	64	72	80
9	0	9	18	27	36	45	54	63	72	81	90
10	0	10	20	30	40	50	60	70	80	90	100

Compare the columns marked 5 and 10 on the multiplication table.

$4 \times 10 = 40$
$4 \times 5 = 20$

$7 \times 10 = 70$
$7 \times 5 = 35$

$9 \times 10 = 90$
$9 \times 5 = 45$

Do you notice a pattern above? To multiply a number by 5, you can first multiply it by 10 and then take half of the product. This strategy works for both odd and even numbers. For example, to multiply 8×10, you can write 8 with a 0 after it. To multiply 8×5, you can write $\frac{1}{2}$ of 8 (which is 4) with a 0 after it. This is because 5 is $\frac{1}{2}$ of 10.

Find these products without looking at a multiplication table. `Algebra`

1. $5 \times 7 = n$
2. $2 \times 5 = x$
3. $6 \times 5 = n$
4. $10 \times 5 = a$
5. $5 \times 6 = n$
6. $5 \times 8 = y$
7. $3 \times 5 = n$
8. $8 \times 5 = b$
9. $5 \times 5 = n$
10. $7 \times 5 = a$
11. $4 \times 5 = x$
12. $9 \times 5 = t$
13. $5 \times 1 = z$
14. $5 \times 9 = n$
15. $5 \times 3 = p$
16. $5 \times 10 = n$

ⓔ Textbook This lesson is available in the *eTextbook*.

×	0	1	2	3	4	5	6	7	8	9	10
0	0	0	0	0	0	0	0	0	0	0	0
1	0	1	2	3	4	5	6	7	8	9	10
2	0	2	4	6	8	10	12	14	16	18	20
3	0	3	6	9	12	15	18	21	24	27	30
4	0	4	8	12	16	20	24	28	32	36	40
5	0	5	10	15	20	25	30	35	40	45	50
6	0	6	12	18	24	30	36	42	48	54	60
7	0	7	14	21	28	35	42	49	56	63	70
8	0	8	16	24	32	40	48	56	64	72	80
9	0	9	18	27	36	45	54	63	72	81	90
10	0	10	20	30	40	50	60	70	80	90	100

You can use what you know about multiplying by 10 to help you multiply by 9. On the multiplication table, compare the 9 and 10 columns.

$7 \times 10 = 70$ $7 \times 9 = 63$

Notice that $70 - 7 = 63$.

$8 \times 10 = 80$ $8 \times 9 = 72$

Notice that $80 - 8 = 72$.

It's another pattern! To multiply a number by 9, multiply the number by 10 then subtract that number from the product.

- To find 7×9, you can find 7×10 then subtract 7.

- To find 8×9, you can find 8×10 then subtract 8.

- What can you do to find 6×9?
  Find 6×10 then subtract 6.

Find each product. Algebra

17. $9 \times 8 = n$
18. $9 \times 7 = t$
19. $7 \times 9 = n$
20. $5 \times 9 = n$
21. $4 \times 9 = f$
22. $9 \times 9 = a$
23. $9 \times 6 = c$
24. $3 \times 9 = n$
25. $6 \times 9 = t$
26. $8 \times 9 = b$
27. $9 \times 1 = n$
28. $9 \times 0 = t$

29. Melinda and Pina collect CDs. At a used CD store Melinda buys 3 CDs for $8 each. Pina buys 2 CDs for $2 each and 3 CDs for $6 each. Who spent more money? How much more?

30. **Extended Response** Reed's Book Barn is having a sale where customers get 1 free book for every 2 books they buy. Rasheed and his sister visit the sale and buy 9 books. How many of those 9 books were free? How much money did they spend on the other books? How do you know?

Key Ideas

Area is the measure of the interior, or inside, of a figure.

There are several different ways to find the area of a square, but one way is certainly the best.

You can count the number of square units inside the square to find there are 64 square cm. That would take a long time!

Can you think of another way to find the area?

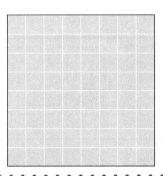

You can count the number of square units along two of the sides. Then multiply those numbers.
8 cm $\times$ 8 cm = 64 cm²

Here is the shortest way. For any square, you can find the length of one side and then multiply that number by itself to find the area. Note that in the answer we write 64 cm² and say *64 square centimeters*.

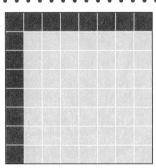

Find the area of each square. **Algebra**

1 A =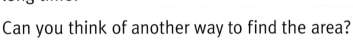

3 cm

2 A =

4 cm

3 A =

7 cm

4 A =

6 cm

e Textbook This lesson is available in the *eTextbook*.

Solve the following.

5 Aiko's table is square-shaped and has a surface area of 36 ft². How long is the table? How wide is it?

6 If the length of one side of a square is 12 m, how long are the other 3 sides?

7 **Extended Response** If you know only the area of a square, how can you find the lengths of the sides? Explain.

8 **Extended Response** Alex and Juanita's uncle gave them 4 dozen 1 ft by 1 ft carpet squares to cover the floor of their tree house. They measured one side of the square-shaped floor and found it was 8 ft long. Will they have enough carpet squares to cover the entire floor? If not, how many more squares will they need?

Draw the image below on graph paper. Use the measurements from the chart in your drawing to find the area of the larger green square.

Algebra

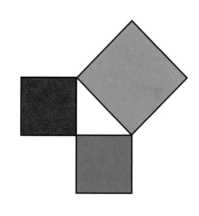

	Length of Side (red square)	Length of Side (blue square)	Area of Square (green square)
9	1 cm	1 cm	
10	2 cm	2 cm	
11	3 cm	3 cm	
12	4 cm	4 cm	
13	5 cm	5 cm	
14	6 cm	6 cm	
15	7 cm	7 cm	

 **Journal**

What do you want to remember about square facts?

Multiplying by 3, 4, 6, and 8

Key Ideas

You can use the facts you already know to help you figure out other facts.

To multiply a number by 4, double that number twice.

So $4 \times 7 = 2 \times 7 + 2 \times 7$ or $14 + 14 = 28$. You may be able to think of other ways you remember the $\times 4$ facts.

For the $\times 3$ facts, you can add the number you are multiplying to its double.
So 3×7 is $14 + 7 = 21$, and 3×8 is $16 + 8 = 24$.

You already know most of the facts involving $\times 6$ and $\times 8$, but these suggestions may also help.

To multiply by 6:

Since 6 is twice 3, you can multiply the number by 3 instead of 6 and double the product. For example:

$$6 \times 7 = n$$

$$3 \times 7 = 21$$

$$21 + 21 = 42$$

To multiply by 8:

Since 8 is twice 4, you can multiply the number by 4 instead of 8 and double the product. For example:

$$8 \times 7 = n$$

$$4 \times 7 = 28$$

$$28 + 28 = 56$$

Multiply to solve for *n*. Algebra

1. $4 \times 3 = n$
2. $4 \times 6 = n$
3. $6 \times 4 = n$
4. $8 \times 4 = n$
5. $3 \times 6 = n$
6. $6 \times 6 = n$
7. $9 \times 4 = n$
8. $6 \times 8 = n$
9. $7 \times 3 = n$
10. $7 \times 6 = n$
11. $8 \times 7 = n$
12. $9 \times 8 = n$
13. $8 \times 3 = n$
14. $8 \times 6 = n$
15. $4 \times 7 = n$
16. $9 \times 3 = n$

e Textbook This lesson is available in the *eTextbook*.

Game

Multiplication Strategies and Practice

Cube 100 Game

Players: Two

Materials: *Number Cubes*: Two 0–5 (red), two 5–10 (blue)

Object: To get the greatest score less than or equal to 100

Math Focus: Adding, multiplying, probability, and mathematical reasoning

HOW TO PLAY

1 Player one roll the cubes one at a time and adds.

2 After any roll, instead of adding that number, a player may multiply it by the sum of the previous numbers. Once a player multiplies, his or her turn is over.

3 The player with the score closer to, but not greater than, 100 wins the round.

SAMPLE GAME

Wendy rolled **6**, then **3**.

$6 + 3 = 9$

Then she rolled **9**.

$9 \times 9 = 81$

She stopped after three rolls.

Wendy's score was 81.

Todd won the round.

Todd rolled **5**, then **5**.

$5 + 5 = 10$

Then he rolled **6**.

$10 + 6 = 16$

He rolled another **6**.
$16 \times 6 = 96$

Todd's score was 96.

Multiplication and Addition Laws

Key Ideas

Using laws relating to addition and multiplication may help you avoid unnecessary work.

You have already discovered that when you add or multiply two numbers, such as m and n, the order makes no difference in the answer.

- For example: $m \times n = n \times m$ and $m + n = n + m$. These facts are called the Commutative Law for multiplication and addition of numbers.

You also know that when you multiply any number (n) by 1, or when you add 0 to any number, the answer is the original number.

- For example: $1 \times n = n \times 1 = n$, and $0 + n = n + 0 = n$. 1 and 0 are called the identity elements for multiplication and addition.

- In multiplication, 0 has an interesting property because when you multiply any number by 0 the product is 0. For instance, for all numbers (n), $0 \times n = n \times 0 = 0$. When used as a factor, 0 is the only number that results in 0 as a product.

If you wish to multiply 12 by 8 you can use 12 as an addend 8 times. To simplify the addition, you can do the following operations: $8 \times 12 = 8 \times (10 + 2) = (8 \times 10) + (8 \times 2) = 80 + 16 = 96$.

- For a, b, and c (or any three numbers), $a \times (b + c) = (a \times b) + (a \times c)$. This is called the Distributive Law for multiplication over addition.

Is it true that $3 + (2 + 1) = (3 + 2) + 1$ and $(2 \times 3) \times 4 = 2 \times (3 \times 4)$? Yes, this fact is called the Associative Law for addition and multiplication of numbers.

- If you have 3 numbers to add or multiply, the following is true: $a + (b + c) = (a + b) + c$ and $(f \times g) \times h = f \times (g \times h)$.

ⓔ Textbook This lesson is available in the *eTextbook*.

Complete the following exercises. Use shortcuts whenever possible.

1. $273 \times 0 = \square$
2. $273 + 0 = \square$
3. $273 \times 1 = \square$
4. $3 \times 80 = \square$
5. $3 \times 3 = \square$
6. $3 \times 83 = \square$
7. $80 \times 5 = \square$
8. $4 \times 5 = \square$
9. $84 \times 5 = \square$
10. $2 \times 30 = \square$
11. $8 \times 2 = \square$
12. $2 \times 38 = \square$
13. $38 + 38 = \square$
14. $83 \times 3 = \square$
15. $84 \times 5 = \square$
16. $76 + 76 = \square$
17. $4 \times 38 = \square$
18. $38 \times 4 = \square$

19. $8 \times 7 \times 6 \times 5 \times 4 \times 3 \times 2 \times 1 \times 0 = \square$
20. $0 \times 1 \times 2 \times 3 \times 4 \times 5 \times 6 \times 7 \times 8 = \square$
21. $(9 + 1) + (8 + 2) + (7 + 3) + (6 + 4) + 5 = \square$
22. $9 + 8 + 7 + 6 + 5 + 4 + 3 + 2 + 1 = \square$

23. Phillip wanted to buy 5 bags of nuts that cost 83¢ each. Help him figure out how much he should pay for all 5 bags.

24. In the school auditorium there are 38 rows of seats. There are 40 seats in each row. How many seats are there altogether? (Hint: Does the answer to Problem 18 help?)

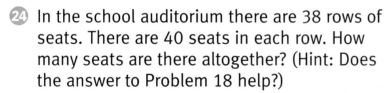

25. Agnes counted the number of seats in the rows of the auditorium in Problem 24 and discovered the front 10 rows had only 39 seats and the back 10 rows had 41 seats. The middle 18 rows had exactly 40 seats, as she had originally thought. How many seats are really in the auditorium?

26. **Extended Response** To find the sum of the numbers from 1 to 100, would you rather use a calculator or solve by hand? Explain.

 **Journal**

Write any useful ideas about shortcuts that were discussed today and whether you think they might help you in the future. Try to give examples of when you might use these shortcuts.

Multiplying by 11 and by 12

Key Ideas

Multiplication facts involving 11 and 12 can be figured out from facts and laws that you know.

When multiplying 0–9 by 11, you will see a pattern. When you are adding both the ones digit and the tens digit are increased by 1 each time you add 11.

- One $11 = 11 \times 1 = 11$
- Two $11s = 11 \times 2 = 22$
- Four $11s = 11 \times 4 = 44$

Another way to solve problems when multiplying by 11 or 12 is by using the Distributive Law.

The distributive law says $a \times (b + c) = (a \times b) + (a \times c)$.

For example:

$3 \times 12 = 3 \times (10 + 2) = (3 \times 10) + (3 \times 2) = 30 + 6 = 36$

Another example is:

$12 \times 11 = 12 \times (10 + 1) = (12 \times 10) + (12 + 1) = 120 + 12 = 132$

Answer the following questions.

1. How many eggs are in 1 dozen?

2. How many eggs are in 3 dozen?

3. A gross is 12 dozen. How many pencils are in 1 gross?

4. How many pencils are there in 11 dozen?

e Textbook This lesson is available in the *eTextbook*.

Answer the following questions.

5 On Monday Mrs. Hulbert sold 5 dozen eggs. How many eggs did she sell?

6 On Wednesday she sold 4 dozen eggs. How many eggs was that?

7 On Friday Mrs. Hulbert sold 3 dozen eggs. How many eggs did she sell over the three days?

8 How many eggs did Mrs. Hulbert sell on Wednesday and Friday?

9 Each football team has 11 members on the field at a time. If 2 teams are playing, how many players are on the field?

SOCIAL STUDIES **10** On Saturday there were 5 different football games being played on 5 different fields. How many players were on the 5 fields?

11 There is going to be a tournament to decide which of 8 football teams is the champion. On the first Saturday the 8 teams will play each other in 4 games. On the second Saturday the winners of the first 4 games will play, and on the third Saturday the winners from the second Saturday will play.

a. **Extended Response** How many games will be played in the tournament to determine the champion? Explain how you got your answer.

b. How many players will be on the fields on the first Saturday?

c. How many players will be on the fields on the second Saturday?

d. How many players will be on the field on the last Saturday?

Give the value of *n* in each of the following.

12 $10 \times 10 = n$

13 $n = 11 \times 11$

14 $11 \times 9 = n$

15 $9 \times 11 = n$

16 $n = 12 \times 12$

17 $7 \times 8 = n$

18 $n = 8 \times 6$

19 $n = 8 \times 12$

20 $11 \times 12 = n$

21 $n \times n = 100$

22 $64 = n \times n$

23 $n = 8 \times 8$

 **Writing + Math** **Journal**

Describe an interesting characteristic about multiples of 11.

Estimating Area

Key Ideas

Estimates for areas of some figures can be made from estimates of length and width measurements.

Amir is thinking of a rectangle. He says, "It can't be less than 4 centimeters long, but it can't be more than 5 centimeters long. It can't be less than 1 centimeter wide, but it can't be more than 2 centimeters wide."

Amir can't be thinking of this rectangle because it is less than 4 centimeters long.

He can't be thinking of this rectangle because it is more than 2 centimeters wide.

He might be thinking of this rectangle.

Could any of these rectangles be the one Amir is thinking of? Write *yes* or *no* for each one. Then use a centimeter ruler to measure.

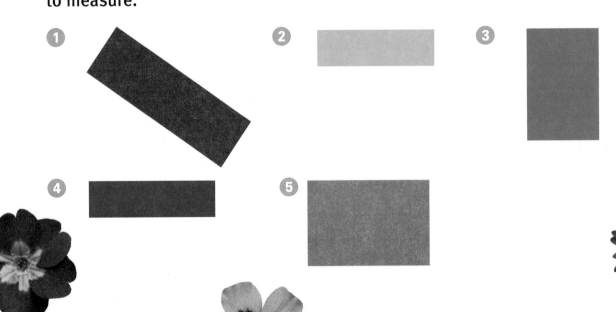

1

2

3

4

5

e Textbook This lesson is available in the *eTextbook*.

Create each drawing described below to answer the following questions.

Onawa and Simon had an argument about whose garden was bigger. They decided to measure them.

Onawa's garden is at least 9 meters long, but not more than 10 meters long. It is at least 6 meters wide, but not more than 7 meters wide.

6 Draw and label a picture of the smallest garden Onawa might have.

7 What is the smallest area Onawa's garden could have?

8 Draw and label a picture of the largest garden Onawa might have.

9 What is the largest area Onawa's garden could have?

Simon's garden is at least 8 meters long, but no more than 9 meters long. It is at least 7 meters wide, but no more than 8 meters wide.

10 Draw and label a picture of the smallest garden Simon might have.

11 What is the smallest area Simon's garden could have?

12 Draw a picture of the largest garden Simon might have.

13 What is the largest area Simon's garden could have?

14 **Extended Response** Can you tell whose garden has the greater area, Onawa's or Simon's? Explain how you found your answer.

Complete the table.

Garden Owner	Length (meters)		Width (meters)		Area (square meters)	
	At Least	No More Than	At Least	No More Than	At Least	No More Than
15 Anita	9	10	4	5	36	
16 Larry	7	8	7	8		
17 Celia	8	9	5	6		
18 Jessie	6	7	5	6		

 **Journal**

Write about how great a variation in area can result when measurements with relatively small variations are multiplied.

Exploring Problem Solving

Jane is helping to buy softballs for the school team. The coach asks her to find the best deal for 20 softballs.

PowerTech Softballs
$6 each
Buy 4— Get a fifth one FREE!

Wallop Softballs
$5 EACH

DURAPLAY Softballs
2 for $11
Get **$15 off** when you buy a dozen!

Jane solved the problem this way:

I realized that there are a lot of different ways to buy 20 softballs. So I decided to Make an Organized Table.

Wallop	Power Tech	Duraplay	Total Cost
20	0	0	$100.00
19	1	0	$101.00
19	0	1	$100.50
18	2	0	$102.00
18	1	1	

Think about Jane's strategy. Answer these questions.

1. Is Jane's total for 19 Wallop softballs and 1 PowerTech softball correct? How do you know?

2. How much would it cost for 1 DuraPlay softball?

3. Look at the last row on the table. Will the total cost be more than or less than $102? How do you know?

4. If Jane continues the pattern in her table, what combination will she write next?

5. Will Jane's strategy work? Why or why not?

6. Would you use Jane's strategy or a different strategy to solve the problem? Explain.

 e Textbook This lesson is available in the *eTextbook*.

Jane decided to Make an Organized Table again.

This time I made a different table so I would not have as many calculations to do.

Number of Softballs	Wallop Cost	Power Tech Cost	Duraplay Cost
1	$5.00	$6.00	$5.50
2	$10.00	$12.00	$11.00
3	$15.00	$18.00	$16.50
4	$20.00	$24.00	$22.00
5	$25.00	$24.00	

Think about the way Jane changed her strategy. Answer these questions.

7 What does the cost of $20 in the second column tell you?

8 What is the least amount you can pay for 5 softballs? How?

9 How far do you think Jane will continue her table?

10 How is this table different from Jane's first table?

11 Do you think Jane's new strategy will solve the problem? Explain.

12 Use any strategy to solve the problem.

Cumulative Review

Multidigit Addition and Subtraction Lesson 2.1–2.3

Find the difference or the sum.

1 87 − 46 = ⬛

2 49 + 73 = ⬛

3 492 + 764 = ⬛

Using Relation Signs Lesson 2.4

Replace each ⬛ with >, <, or =.

4 475 ⬛ 389

5 562 ⬛ 562

6 275 ⬛ 257

Estimating with Maps and Charts Lesson 1.1, 1.9

Use the table below to answer the following questions.

Population Growth of Three States			
State	1980	1990	2000
Iowa	2,913,808	2,776,755	2,926,324
Kentucky	3,660,324	3,685,296	4,041,769
Nevada	800,508	1,201,833	1,998,257

7 Which state had the greatest population in 1980? In 1990?

8 Name the state or states that had a greater population in 2000 than in 1990.

Approximation Applications Lesson 2.6

Select an approximate answer for the following problems.

9 Two years is approximately how many days?

Ⓐ 600   Ⓑ 700   Ⓒ 800

10 A dictionary has about 20 words on each page and has about 300 pages. How many words are defined in that dictionary?

Ⓐ 6,000   Ⓑ 60,000 Ⓒ 600

ⓔ **Textbook** This lesson is available in the *eTextbook.*

Integers Lesson 2.8

Complete the table to determine each contestant's score.

Contestant's Scores

	Name	Question 1	Question 2	Question 3	Question 4	Question 5	Total Score
11	Natalie	2	2	2	−1	2	
12	Jo Ellen	2	2	−1	−1	2	
13	DeShawn	−1	2	2	2	2	
14	Jaquie	−1	−1	2	−1	2	

Rounding Lesson 1.4

Round these numbers to the nearest hundred.

15 589

16 3,821

17 7,053

Subtraction with Hidden Digits Lesson 2.5

Find the missing digit.

18
$$\begin{array}{r} 4\ 0\ 7 \\ -\ 2\ 2\ 9 \\ \hline 1\ \_\ 8 \end{array}$$

19
$$\begin{array}{r} 6\ 0\ 2 \\ -\ 3\ 4\ 5 \\ \hline 2\ 5\ \_ \end{array}$$

20
$$\begin{array}{r} 3\ 2\ 1 \\ -\ 2\ 8\ 5 \\ \hline \_\ 6 \end{array}$$

Multiplying Lesson 3.1 – 3.7

Multiply to solve for n.

21 $12 \times 6 = n$ 22 $3 \times 12 = n$ 23 $11 \times 5 = n$ 24 $10 \times 11 = n$

25 $3 \times 11 = n$ 26 $12 \times 4 = n$ 27 $6 \times 11 = n$ 28 $8 \times 12 = n$

Finding Missing Factors

Key Ideas

Multiplication and division are inverse operations.

For example, in the equation $24 \div n = 8$, $n = 3$ because $8 \times 3 = 24$. The letter n stands for a missing factor.

There are different ways to find missing factors. Remember what you learned about finding missing addends in Lesson 1.8.

Mia's class is doing the Missing Factor Activity.

$$3 \times n = 15$$

Pak has the number 5 on his back because $3 \times 5 = 15$, so $n = 5$. *Think 3 times what equals 15.* Guess and check until you find the answer.

$$3 \times 3 = 9 \longleftrightarrow 3 \times 4 = 12 \longleftrightarrow 3 \times 5 = 15$$

Write the number that Mia has on her back.　**Algebra**

	Pak's Number	Mia's Number	The Product Is
1	4	▢	36
2	7	▢	49
3	10	▢	10
4	1	▢	8
5	0	▢	0

6 **Extended Response** Look at Problem 5 again. Can you tell which number Mia has? What numbers might she have? Explain.

e Textbook This lesson is available in the *eTextbook.*

Use the equations on the right to help you answer the following questions.

7 A machine at Dough-Boyz Donuts cuts holes in the middle of 9 doughnuts every minute. How many minutes will it take the machine to cut holes in 90 doughnuts?

$n \times 9 = 90$

8 Jorge made 8 trips around the park on his bike. He rode a total of 24 kilometers. How long is each trip around the park?

$8 \times n = 24$

9 Gina earns $5 each time she mows her aunt's lawn. How many times will she have to mow the lawn to earn the $35 she needs for a new tennis racquet?

$n \times 5 = 35$

10 Grant had $15 when he went to the ball game. He had $6 when he got home. How much did he spend?

$15 - n = 6$

11 Each day Kathy listens to her radio for 4 hours. A battery will power the radio for about 36 hours of listening. For about how many days can Kathy listen to her radio before the battery goes dead?

$4 \times n = 36$

12 Jared baked 24 cookies. He takes 3 cookies in his lunch every day. For how many days will he have cookies in his lunch?

$3 \times n = 24$

13 Tim works 15 hours each week at the pizza shop. If he works the same amount of time on each of 3 days during the week, how many hours must he work each day?

$3 \times n = 15$

Answer the following questions.

14 Each day Craig knits 10 centimeters of the scarf he's making. He wants the scarf to be 1 meter (100 centimeters) long. How many days will it take Craig to make his scarf?

15 Every day Tanya uses 4 slices of bread for her lunch sandwiches. A loaf of bread has 16 slices. If Tanya has 3 loaves of bread, how many days can she make sandwiches?

16 Marcia is inviting 28 friends to her birthday party.

   a. She has 4 days to write all the invitations. If she writes 6 invitations each day, will she finish in time?

   b. If she writes 7 invitations each day, will she finish in time?

   c. If she writes 8 invitations each day, will she finish in time?

Solve for *n*. 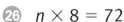 Algebra

17 $9 \times n = 27$

18 $n \times 10 = 60$

19 $6 \times n = 30$

20 $3 \times n = 0$

21 $72 = 9 \times n$

22 $n \times 6 = 54$

23 $48 = 8 \times n$

24 $7 \times n = 42$

25 $6 \times n = 48$

26 $n \times 8 = 72$

e Textbook This lesson is available in the *eTextbook*.

27 Raulito has $87 in his bank account. He wants to deposit enough money to bring his balance to exactly $100. How much money should he deposit?

28 Jacob has already driven 87 miles of a 100-mile trip. How many more miles must he drive?

29 Juanita needs 100 coupons to collect a prize. She already has 87 coupons. How many more coupons does she need?

30 **Extended Response** Do you notice anything about the first three problems on this page?

31 Richard needs 45 hats for a party. Hats come 5 to a package. How many packages of hats does he need?

32 Ed had $150 in his bank account. He wrote a check, but he forgot to write down the amount. He called the bank and found out that he has $126 in his account. For what amount was the check written?

33 Mañuel had a balance of $250 in his checking account. He wrote one check for $20. Then he wrote another check, but forgot to record the amount. How much money is left in his bank account?

34 Nina's class has finished 38 lessons in their geography book. The book has 112 lessons. How many more lessons must the class complete to finish the book?

35 Ricardo's long-distance plan allows him to make calls for 4¢ a minute. If he talks long-distance for 5 minutes on Monday and Tuesday, 9 minutes on Wednesday, and 3 minutes on Thursday, how long can he talk on Friday so that he only spends $1 on long-distance calls for the week?

Multiplication and Division

Key Ideas

Multiplication and division can help solve everyday problems.

When you solved missing-term problems in the previous lesson, you were getting ready for division. Multiplication and division are inverse operations. Just as subtraction undoes addition division undoes multiplication.

$8 + 6 = 14$, so $14 - 6 = 8$ $8 \times 6 = 48$, so $48 \div 6 = 8$

$56 = 7 \times 8$, so $56 \div 8 = 7$ $49 = 7 \times 7$, so $7 = 49 \div 7$

Sometimes we compute division using this symbol: $\overline{)}$

For example: $7\overline{)56}$

This means we are going to divide 56 by 7. Write the answer as shown:

$$7\overline{)56}^{\,8}$$

Remember, the answer to a division problem is called a quotient.

Solve each problem. SOCIAL STUDIES

1. Alonzo earns $4 each hour at his job. Today he earned $20. How many hours did he work today?

2. **Extended Response** If you knew only the number of hours Alonzo worked and how much he earned, what would you do to find out how much he makes each hour? Explain.

3. Maria has to work only 2 hours to earn $12. How much would she earn at the end of a 3-day work week if she works 5 hours each day?

4. If 8 children want to share 24 cookies equally, how many cookies should each child get?

e Textbook This lesson is available in the *eTextbook.*

Solve each problem.

5. Patrick and his friends like to play football in the backyard. They have two teams, the Ravens and the Hawks. They give each other 7 points for each touchdown since they do not have anywhere to kick extra points or field goals. After playing for an hour the Ravens had scored 42 points. How many touchdowns did they score?

6. What was the least number of touchdowns the Hawks needed in order to have more points than the Ravens?

7. The Hawks came from behind to win. At the end of the game the final score was 56 to 49.

   a. How many touchdowns did the winning team score?

   b. How many touchdowns did the losing team score?

   c. By how many touchdowns did the Hawks win?

Divide. Solve for *n*. Algebra

8. $10 \div 10 = n$

9. $72 \div 9 = n$

10. $63 \div 7 = n$

11. $20 \div 5 = n$

12. $35 \div 7 = n$

13. $n = 56 \div 8$

14. $n = 5 \div 1$

15. $72 \div 8 = n$

16. $64 \div 8 = n$

17. $n = 14 \div 7$

18. $60 \div 6 = n$

19. $80 \div 10 = n$

20. $42 \div 7 = n$

21. $n = 30 \div 5$

22. $n = 25 \div 5$

Find each quotient.

23. $5\overline{)50}$

24. $7\overline{)63}$

25. $10\overline{)90}$

26. $5\overline{)30}$

27. $8\overline{)16}$

28. $3\overline{)21}$

29. $5\overline{)40}$

30. $1\overline{)2}$

Writing + Math **Journal**

Explain how you can use your estimation skills and the fact that multiplication and division are inverse operations to solve a division problem on a multiple-choice test.

Key Ideas

Sometimes you cannot divide a quantity equally.

A remainder is the number that is left over after dividing.

For example:

There are 7 children who want to divide 56¢ equally. How much will each child get?

$$\begin{array}{r} 8 \\ 7\overline{)56} \end{array}$$

If 7 children want to divide 57¢ equally, how much will each child get?

$$7\overline{)57}$$

After each child gets 8 pennies, there is still 1 penny left over. Sometimes we wish to divide a whole number of things equally but cannot do so without having something left over, or remaining.

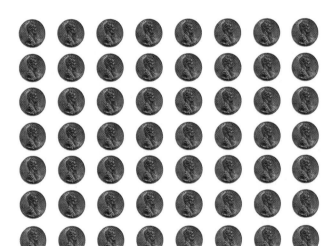

We can write:

$$\begin{array}{r} 8R1 \\ 7\overline{)57} \\ -56 \\ \hline 1 \end{array}$$

$8 \times 7 = 56$

$57 - 56 = 1$

When we read the answer we say, *8 remainder 1,* or *8 and 1 left over.*

If 6 children want to divide 40 cents equally, how much will each child get? How much will be left over?

$$\begin{array}{r} 6R4 \\ 6\overline{)40} \\ -36 \\ \hline 4 \end{array}$$

$6 \times 6 = 36 \qquad 40 - 36 = 4$

Each child gets 6 cents, and there are 4 cents remaining.

eTextbook This lesson is available in the *eTextbook.*

It is important to know the parts of a division problem.

$$\overset{quotient}{divisor)\overline{dividend}}$$

- You already know the answer is called the quotient.
- The dividend is the number that is to be divided.
- The divisor is the number the dividend is to be divided by.

Divide. Watch for remainders.

1. 8)48
2. 8)51
3. 9)54
4. 9)58
5. 5)37

6. 7)43
7. 3)26
8. 10)46
9. 3)29
10. 6)36

11. 5)47
12. 6)63
13. 8)34
14. 5)45
15. 7)54

Answer these questions.

Sasha, Tina, Nikia, and Liza hunted for treasure on the beach. When they found valuable things the girls sold them. Sometimes they found money. At the end of each week they divided the money equally.

16. During the first week the girls found some shells and coral. They sold these for $27. They also found $5 in cash.

   a. How much money did they get altogether?

   b. How much money should each girl get?

17. During the third week they found some driftwood and three old bottles. They sold these for $23. They also found $7 in cash.

   a. How much money did they have altogether?

   b. How much money should each girl get?

18. **Extended Response** In real life when is it impossible to solve a division problem without a remainder? Give an example and explain it.

Key Ideas

Factors are numbers you multiply to get the product.
In the multiplication fact $3 \times 6 = 18$, 3 and 6 are factors of 18.

A multiple of a whole number is the product of that number and any whole number. If $a \times b = n$, then a and b are factors of n and n is a multiple of b and a. For example, in $3 \times 6 = 18$, 3 and 6 are factors of 18, and 18 is a multiple of 3 and a multiple of 6.

You can call 18 a common multiple of 3 and 6 because it is a multiple of both numbers.

Be sure not to confuse common multiples with common factors. The factors of 3 are 1 and 3 because those are the only two numbers you can multiply to get a product of 3. The factors of 6 are 1, 2, 3, and 6.

You can call 3 a common factor of 3 and 6 because it is a factor of both numbers.

Work with a partner to find the first three common multiples of each pair of numbers.

1. 3 and 7
2. 5 and 9
3. 5 and 4
4. 2 and 3
5. 9 and 8
6. 8 and 5
7. 6 and 10
8. 2 and 8
9. 9 and 12
10. 5 and 10
11. 6 and 9
12. 8 and 12

eTextbook This lesson is available in the *eTextbook*.

The **least common multiple** is the smallest multiple a set of numbers share. For example, the least common multiple of 6 and 9 is 18.

The first seven multiples of 6 are 6, 12, **18**, 24, 30, 36, and 42.

The first seven multiples of 9 are 9, **18**, 27, 36, 45, 54, and 63.

The **greatest common factor** is the greatest factor a pair of numbers shares. For example, the greatest common factor of 14 and 21 is 7.

Factors of 14 are 1, 2, **7,** and 14.

Factors of 21 are 1, 3, **7,** and 21.

Answer the following questions.

13 **Extended Response** What seems to be true of the first common multiple of each of the pairs listed in Problems 1–6? What seems to be true of the second common multiple of all of the pairs?

14 **Extended Response** In what way are the first common multiples for Problems 7–12 different from those for Problems 1–6?

15 Look at Exercises 1–6. Is there any whole number greater than 1 that divides exactly into both

    a. 3 and 7?   **b.** 5 and 9?

    c. 5 and 4?   **d.** 2 and 3?

    e. 9 and 8?   **f.** 8 and 5?

16 Look at Problems 7–12. What is the greatest common factor of the following:

    a. 2 and 8?   **b.** 9 and 12?

    c. 5 and 10?   **d.** 6 and 9?

    e. 8 and 12?

17 **Extended Response** Try to find an interesting pattern for Problems 7–12. Describe the pattern using words or numbers.

18 Think of other pairs of numbers. Predict what their least common multiple will be. Work with your group to check your prediction.

Parentheses

Key Ideas

Sometimes math problems can be solved in different ways.
You have been taught to solve problems going from left to right; however, parentheses can determine which part of a problem is solved first.

The Veterinarians' Assistants

Brenda and her friends like to help Celine, the veterinarian, by volunteering at the dog shelter where Celine works.

"May we help feed your dogs?" the children asked.

"Yes," said Celine. "But first I have to mix some medicine in with their food. You can help me figure out how much medicine to mix in. How much is $4 \times 3 + 2$?"

"It's 14," said Brenda, Jamal, and Cindy.

"No, it's 20," said Elise and Aaron.

The children argued about which answer was right, but they could not decide. Finally Cindy said, "Why don't you explain the whole problem?"

"It doesn't seem like a hard problem," Celine said. "I have to give 4 pills to each dog. I have 3 black dogs and 2 brown dogs. That is $4 \times 3 + 2$, right?"

"Now we know what the correct answer is!" they all said. "It's 20."

ⓔTextbook This lesson is available in the *eTextbook.*

In order to solve a problem with more than one expression, do the operations inside the parentheses first, then work from left to right.

Examples:

a. $40 \div (5 + 3) = 40 \div 8 = 5$

b. $(40 \div 5) + 3 = 8 + 3 = 11$

c. $12 - (8 - 3) = 12 - 5 = 7$

d. $(12 - 8) - 3 = 4 - 3 = 1$

e. $7 \times (5 + 4) = 7 \times 9 = 63$

f. $(7 \times 5) + 4 = 35 + 4 = 39$

g. $32 \div (8 \div 2) = 32 \div 4 = 8$

h. $(32 \div 8) \div 2 = 4 \div 2 = 2$

Solve for *n*. Pay attention to the parentheses and the signs.

1 $24 \div (6 \div 2) = n$

2 $(24 \div 6) \div 2 = n$

3 $28 - (8 \div 4) = n$

4 $(28 - 8) \div 4 = n$

5 $7 \times (4 + 6) = n$

6 $(7 \times 4) + 6 = n$

7 $16 + (7 + 5) = n$

8 $(16 + 7) + 5 = n$

9 $(56 \div 8) + 4 = n$

Solve the following problems.

10 There were 16 people at a party. At 5:30, 2 people left. Two hours later, 3 times as many people left. How many people were still at the party?

11 The host wanted to buy pizza for everyone who was still at the party. A large pizza feeds 4 people. How many pizzas should he buy?

For each problem below, list all of the different answers you can get by putting parentheses in different places. The first two have been done for you.

$5 + 4 \times 3 = n$

$2 \times 10 \div 2 = n$

12 $17 - 10 + 1 = n$

13 $2 \times 3 + 4 = n$

14 $4 \times 6 \div 3 = n$

15 $16 + 3 \times 2 = n$

16 $16 \div 4 \times 2 = n$

17 $16 - 4 \times 2 = n$

18 $2 \times 3 \times 4 = n$

19 $12 - 2 \times 6 = n$

20 $12 - 2 \times 3 = n$

21 $8 + 12 \div 2 = n$

22 **Extended Response** Make your own exercise. Choose three numbers and two different operations. Put some of the numbers in parentheses. Find the answer. Then explain in your own words how the parentheses led you to your answer.

e Textbook This lesson is available in the *eTextbook*.

Parentheses can tell us which operation to do first. However, some long math problems use more than one set of parentheses. So, people sometimes use other conventions to decide in which order to do the operations.

The rule many people use is to do the operations from left to right.

$$3 + 7 \times 6 - 5 + 4 = 10 \times 6 - 5 + 4 = 60 - 5 + 4 = 55 + 4 = 59$$

One rule, used in algebra, tells us to do all the multiplication and division problems first, and then do the addition and subtraction problems.

$$3 + (7 \times 6) - 5 + 4 = 3 + 42 - 5 + 4 = 45 - 1 = 44$$

A third possible solution would be to do all of the addition and subtraction problems first, and then do the multiplication and division problems.

$$(3 + 7) \times (6 - 5) + 4 = 10 \times 5 = 50$$

Use each of the three rules and a calculator, if necessary, to solve the following problems. You might discover that two or three of your answers are the same. Sometimes none of your answers will match. Try to predict which answers will be the same before doing the problems. **Algebra**

23. $8 + 7 \times 6 - 4 = n$

24. $20 - 3 \times 4 + 6 + 2 \times 8 = n$

25. $2 \times 3 \times 4 + 8 = n$

26. $2 \times 3 \times 4 + 8 \times 5 = n$

27. $2 + 3 + 4 \times 8 = n$

28. $2 + 3 + 4 \times 8 + 2 = n$

29. $3 \times 4 + 7 = n$

30. $3 + 4 \times 7 = n$

31. $2 \times 3 \times 4 \times 5 = n$

32. $2 + 3 + 4 + 5 = n$

33. $2 \times 3 + 4 \times 5 = n$

34. $2 + 3 \times 4 + 5 = n$

35. $2 \times 3 \times 4 + 5 = n$

36. $2 + 3 + 4 \times 5 = n$

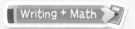 **Journal**

Explain why you think math rules in regards to operations are important.

Key Ideas

You can apply what you've learned about adding, subtracting, multiplying, and dividing to solve different kinds of problems.

Use any problem-solving methods that work for you, such as drawing pictures or identifying missing information.

Read each problem carefully, and then solve it. Think about which operations to use.

1 Mike received $24.75 on his birthday. Three days later he got a birthday card with $5 in it. How much money did Mike receive for his birthday altogether?

2 **Extended Response** The Lazy Z Ranch is 5 kilometers wide. What is the area of the ranch? How can you tell? Explain.

3 Melissa has 35 customers on her paper route. She began her route with 35 papers and now she has 10 left. How many papers has she delivered?

4 Last spring the Ecology Club planted 108 tree seedlings. Of those, 19 seedlings didn't survive the winter. How many trees made it through the winter?

5 Leilani can ride 1 kilometer on her bike in about 4 minutes. About how long will it take her to ride to Echo Lake, a distance of 8 kilometers?

6 Billy's rectangular tree house is 4 feet long, 7 feet tall, and 8 feet wide. What is the perimeter of the tree house's floor?

7 Mr. and Mrs. Kuhn and their 2 children ate lunch in the cafeteria at the science museum. They shared a $3 jumbo order of french fries, and each person ordered a sandwich for $5. How much did they spend on lunch altogether?

8 Amanda has invited 26 people to a party. She wants to give each person a party hat. Hats come in packages of 10. How many packages does she need to buy?

e **Textbook** This lesson is available in the *eTextbook*.

Mental Math

Cubo Game

Players: Two or more

Materials: *Number Cubes*:
two 0–5 (red), two 5–10 (blue)

Object: To score as close to 21 as possible

Math Focus: Mental math with all four operations

HOW TO PLAY

1 Roll all four cubes on each turn.

2 Use any combination of the four operations (addition, subtraction, multiplication, and division) on the numbers rolled. Use the number on each cube exactly once. If two cubes have the same number, you must use the numbers twice.

3 The player who scores exactly 21, or closest to it, is the winner of the round.

SAMPLE GAME

If you rolled	You could get	By doing these operations
	19	6 − 3 = 3; 3 × 6 = 18 ; 18 + 1 = 19
3 6	23	3 × 6 = 18; 18 + 6 = 24 ; 24 − 1 = 23
6 1	21	6 − 1 = 5; 5 × 3 = 15 ; 15 + 6 = 21
	21	6 − 3 = 3; 6 + 1 = 7 ; 3 × 7 = 21

Another Way to Play this Game

Make the goal a number other than 21.

If your picker-uppers have ever let you down, then you will want to take a look at what some towel-testing students in Wisconsin have done. They compared five brands of paper towels and published their report on the Internet site of the National Student Research Center.

To find out whether you get what you pay for, these students tested each brand to see how much water it could hold and how much weight it could support.

So, what is the verdict? You be the judge. The students carefully designed two types of tests.

Absorbency Test

- We took a measuring cup and filled it to 250 mL. We then put the paper towel into the measuring cup.

- After ten seconds we removed the paper towel and let the excess water drip off into the container.

- Then we measured how much water was left. (Take what is left in the measuring cup, and subtract it from 250 mL. That is how much the towel absorbed.)

- We did this three times with each paper towel.

Strength Tests

Strength when Wet

- First, we wet the paper towel. Then we wrung out the excess water and put the paper towel on a hard surface.

- Next, we added weights and lifted the paper towel off the surface.

- If the paper towel held the weights, we gradually added more weights, until the paper towel ripped.

- We did this test three times with each paper towel.

Strength when Dry

- We used the same procedure, except we didn't wet the paper towel.

These are the results that the students reported:

Brand	Sheets in 1 Roll	Price of 1 Roll	Water Absorbed (milliliters)	Wet Strength (grams)	Dry Strength (grams)		
A	55	$0.97	65	327	1,801	1,970	2,141
B	78	$0.69	25	270	1,148	1,078	1,178
C	50	$1.29	70	1,078	3,471	3,571	3,301
D	64	$0.97	50	449	2,648	2,698	2,648
E	52	$0.59	32	1,225	2,448	2,698	2,648

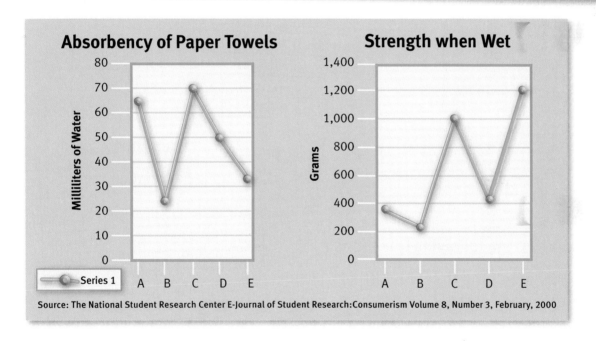

Source: The National Student Research Center E-Journal of Student Research: Consumerism Volume 8, Number 3, February, 2000

Solve these problems.

1 Which brand costs the most for each sheet? Which brand costs the least for each sheet? How can you tell without making any calculations?

2 Why didn't the students do each test just once? Does the report show all the test results?

3 What do you find most useful about the tests and the way the results are shown?

4 If you were designing the tests and reporting the results, what would you do differently?

Exploring Problem Solving

Imagine you work for a baseball team and are in charge of testing three different brands of bats: Arrow Bats, Champ Bats, and Slugger Bats. One of your workers has completed a few tests and gave you this report.

Hitting Tests

Test	Description	Results
1	I asked every doctor in town which bat they liked best.	Three doctors thought Slugger was best, one said Arrow looked the nicest, and two liked Champ. The other fifty-four said they did not know about bats or said they did not want to be bothered.
2	I practiced hitting with each bat and kept a record of my hits and misses.	Slugger: Missed all 10 pitches Arrow: Missed 23 pitches, then hit a ball that hopped slowly to the pitcher Champ: Missed all 17 pitches
3	I gave each brand of bat to a different hitter on the team for two weeks.	<table><tr><th>Player</th><th>Bat</th><th>At Bats</th><th>Hits</th></tr><tr><td>Sandy</td><td>Slugger</td><td>41</td><td>12</td></tr><tr><td>Al</td><td>Arrow</td><td>40</td><td>15</td></tr><tr><td>Chad</td><td>Champ</td><td>8</td><td>5</td></tr></table>

Strength Tests

Test	Description	Results
1	I hit each bat against a rock.	None of the bats broke.
2	I found a wrecking crew that was tearing down a building. I asked them to try to break all the bats using the huge steel ball that swung from a crane.	All the bats broke.

Answer the following questions.

5 Why aren't the first two hitting tests good tests?

6 Who do you think did the best hitting in the third test? Explain.

7 Does the third hitting test tell you which bat is best for getting hits? Explain.

8 Do you think that the two strength tests show that all three brands have the same strength? Explain.

9 Design your own tests for bats. First decide what features of the bats you will test. Then describe the exact method you will use to test each feature and how you will judge which bat is best overall.

e Textbook This lesson is available in the *eTextbook*.

Cumulative Review

Using Maps and Charts Lesson 1.9, 2.6

Use the table to choose the best answers below.

1 About how much farther is it from Lisbon to New York than from Lisbon to St. John's?

Ⓐ about 1,500 km

Ⓑ about 3,000 km

Ⓒ not enough information

Distances from New York City, United States	
City and Country	Distance (in kilometers)
Istanbul, Turkey	8,072
Lisbon, Portugal	5,424
Paris, France	5,838
St. John's, Canada	1,842
Shanghai, China	11,881

2 About how much farther is it from to New York to Istanbul than from New York to Paris?

Ⓐ about 1,500 km

Ⓑ about 3,000 km

Ⓒ about 5,000 km

3 About how much farther is it from New York to Shanghai than from New York to Lisbon?

Ⓐ about 6,500 km

Ⓑ about 7,000 km

Ⓒ about 7,500 km

· ·

Multidigit Addition and Subtraction Lessons 2.1–2.2

Add or subtract.

4
$$\begin{array}{r} 33 \\ + 21 \\ \hline \end{array}$$

5
$$\begin{array}{r} 56 \\ - 23 \\ \hline \end{array}$$

6
$$\begin{array}{r} 5697 \\ + 3425 \\ \hline \end{array}$$

7
$$\begin{array}{r} 4821 \\ - 3962 \\ \hline \end{array}$$

8
$$\begin{array}{r} 796 \\ - 489 \\ \hline \end{array}$$

9
$$\begin{array}{r} 1800 \\ + 212 \\ \hline \end{array}$$

10
$$\begin{array}{r} 1642 \\ + 1999 \\ \hline \end{array}$$

11
$$\begin{array}{r} 700 \\ - 364 \\ \hline \end{array}$$

12
$$\begin{array}{r} 15633 \\ - 13992 \\ \hline \end{array}$$

13
$$\begin{array}{r} 1492 \\ + 1776 \\ \hline \end{array}$$

Cumulative Review

Multiplying Lesson 3.1-3.7

Multiply to solve for *n*.

⑭ $6 \times 6 = n$ **⑮** $8 \times 3 = n$ **⑯** $4 \times 11 = n$ **⑰** $11 \times 7 = n$

Multidigit Addition and Subtraction Lesson 2.3

Solve these problems.

⑱ Yesterday Sabina bought a bicycle for $98. Today she bought a basket for it for $13. How much did she spend in all?

⑲ Mrs. Moran bought 11 apples, 13 oranges, 17 bananas, and 26 carrots. How many more pieces of fruit than vegetables did she buy?

⑳ Jane bought the same kind of bicycle with a basket for $109. Who paid less for her bicycle and her basket?

Addition and Subtraction with Hidden Digits Lesson 2.5

Choose the correct answer.

㉑
$$\begin{array}{r} 7\,0\,\square \\ +\,3\,\square\,5 \end{array}$$
Ⓐ 917   Ⓑ 1076   Ⓒ 1194   Ⓓ 425

㉒
$$\begin{array}{r} 4\,7\,\square \\ -\,\square\,\square\,\square \end{array}$$
Ⓐ 504   Ⓑ 484   Ⓒ 319   Ⓓ 670

Integers Lesson 2.8

Write the integer for each point on the number line.

```
        B        A           D C                        E
◄──┼┼┼┼┼┼┼┼┼┼┼┼┼┼┼┼┼┼┼┼┼┼┼┼┼┼┼┼┼┼┼┼──►
                          0
```

㉓ E   **㉔** A   **㉕** D

㉖ B   **㉗** C

Key Ideas Review

In this chapter you reviewed multiplication and division facts and explored how to use these operations to reduce your work.

You learned various properties of multiplication and addition.

You learned how to find factors and common multiples of numbers.

Match the law to the example demonstrating it.

Associative Law	Distributive Law	Commutative Law

1 $m \times n = n \times m$

2 $a + (b + c) = (a + b) + c$

3 $a \times (b + c) = (a \times b) + (a \times c)$

Solve the following:

4 **Extended Response** How can repeated addition help find the answer to a multiplication problem? Provide an example.

5 **Extended Response** How can repeated subtraction help find the answer to a division problem?

6 What does it mean to square a number?

7 What is a remainder?

8 $12 - 6 + (8 \times 7) = $ ▨

9 $(4 - 2) \times 12 \div 3 = $ ▨

10 $(9 \div 3) \times 7 + 5 = $ ▨

Lessons 3.1–3.7 **Multiply** to solve for *n*.

1. $4 \times 4 = n$

2. $11 \times 6 = n$

3. $n = 12 \times 3$

4. $n = 4 \times 6$

5. $0 \times 11 = n$

6. $n = 6 \times 8$

Answer the following questions.

7. Andrew bought 3 pencils for 9¢ each at a department store. How much did they cost altogether?

A shirt costs $22. A tie costs $8.

8. How much do 2 shirts cost?

9. How much do 2 shirts and 4 ties cost?

Lesson 3.8 10. Patricia's patio is a square. Its area is between 40 and 50 square meters. The length of each side is a whole number of meters.

    a. What is the length of each side of the patio?

    b. What is the perimeter of the patio?

Lesson 3.10 11. Tad paid 72¢ for eight erasers at the school bookstore. How much did each eraser cost?

12. David paid 80¢ for 2 writing tablets. How much did each tablet cost?

Lesson 3.11 13. $7\overline{)37}$ 14. $9\overline{)40}$ 15. $8\overline{)47}$

16. Teresa has 47 stickers to give to 5 children.

    a. How many stickers will each child get?

    b. How many stickers will be left over?

e Textbook This lesson is available in the *eTextbook*.

Lesson 3.12

Solve each problem.

17 Which of the following numbers is a common multiple of 5 and 7?

    a. 12   **b.** 28

    c. 14   **d.** 35

18 Which of the following numbers is *not* a common multiple of 4 and 6?

    a. 12   **b.** 18

    c. 24   **d.** 36

19 Which of the following sets of numbers are factors of 24?

    a. 6 and 10   **b.** 3 and 9

    c. 4 and 8   **d.** 12 and 16

20 Which of the following numbers is *not* a factor of 24?

    a. 18   **b.** 6

    c. 12   **d.** 24

Lesson 3.13

Solve for *n*.

21 $n = 5 + (3 \times 4)$

22 $n = 4 \times (3 - 1)$

23 $8 \times (2 + 7) = n$

24 $(17 - 9) - 5 = n$

Lesson 3.14

25 **Extended Response** Mrs. Sandina knows that the area of her rectangular rug is between 50 and 60 square meters and that the length of the rug is 9 meters. She also knows that the width is a whole number of meters. What is the width? Is there more than one answer? Explain how you got your answer.

26 **Extended Response** Arturo's team, the Bears, played Ahmed's team, the Lions, in football. The Lions scored 7 touchdowns and made 2 field goals. The Bears scored 6 touchdowns. A touchdown is worth 6 points and a field goal is worth 3 points. If the Lions won the game by 3 points, how many field goals did the Bears make? Explain your answer.

Find each product or quotient.

1. $9 \times 6 = $ ☐
   - Ⓐ 54
   - Ⓑ 36
   - Ⓒ 63
   - Ⓓ 41

2. $8 \times 7 = $ ☐
   - Ⓐ 66
   - Ⓑ 56
   - Ⓒ 64
   - Ⓓ none of the above

3. $9 \times 4 = $ ☐
   - Ⓐ 34
   - Ⓑ 40
   - Ⓒ 36
   - Ⓓ 60

4. $5 \times 8 = $ ☐
   - Ⓐ 30
   - Ⓑ 24
   - Ⓒ 42
   - Ⓓ none of the above

5. $3 \times 7 = $ ☐
   - Ⓐ 14
   - Ⓑ 22
   - Ⓒ 21
   - Ⓓ none of the above

6. $64 \div 8 = $ ☐
   - Ⓐ 7
   - Ⓑ 9
   - Ⓒ 6
   - Ⓓ 8

7. $27 \div 9 = $ ☐
   - Ⓐ 4
   - Ⓑ 5
   - Ⓒ 2
   - Ⓓ 3

8. $63 \div 7 = $ ☐
   - Ⓐ 9
   - Ⓑ 8
   - Ⓒ 6
   - Ⓓ none of the above

9. $45 \div 9 = $ ☐
   - Ⓐ 4
   - Ⓑ 8
   - Ⓒ 5
   - Ⓓ 7

10. $50 \div 10 = $ ☐
    - Ⓐ 0
    - Ⓑ 5
    - Ⓒ 10
    - Ⓓ 40

11. $10\overline{)16} = $ ☐
    - Ⓐ 6
    - Ⓑ 1 R6
    - Ⓒ 7 R2
    - Ⓓ 7

12. $9\overline{)38} = $ ☐
    - Ⓐ 4
    - Ⓑ 5
    - Ⓒ 4 R2
    - Ⓓ 4 R6

13. $7\overline{)42} = $ ☐
    - Ⓐ 6
    - Ⓑ 6R2
    - Ⓒ 5 R2
    - Ⓓ 7

14. $24 \div (6 \div 2) = $ ☐
    - Ⓐ 2
    - Ⓑ 8
    - Ⓒ 6
    - Ⓓ 4

15. $(7 \times 4) + 6 = $ ☐
    - Ⓐ 70
    - Ⓑ 17
    - Ⓒ 34
    - Ⓓ 40

16. $(18 \div 6) \times 5 = $ ☐
    - Ⓐ 10
    - Ⓑ 8
    - Ⓒ 12
    - Ⓓ 15

ⓔ **Textbook** This lesson is available in the *eTextbook*.

Solve for *n*.

17. $n \times 8 = 24$

    Ⓐ $n = 4$ Ⓑ $n = 3$

    Ⓒ $n = 5$ Ⓓ $n = 6$

18. $81 \div 9 = n$

    Ⓐ $n = 10$ Ⓑ $n = 9$

    Ⓒ $n = 8$ Ⓓ $n = 7$

19. $n + 8 = 17$

    Ⓐ $n = 8$ Ⓑ $n = 7$

    Ⓒ $n = 10$ Ⓓ none of the above

Answer the following questions.

20. Which of the following numbers is a common factor of 56 and 63?

    Ⓐ 6   Ⓑ 7

    Ⓒ 8   Ⓓ 9

21. Which of the following numbers is a common multiple of 16 and 24?

    Ⓐ 16   Ⓑ 32

    Ⓒ 48   Ⓓ 64

22. What is the greatest common factor of 18 and 24?

    Ⓐ 9   Ⓑ 3

    Ⓒ 6   Ⓓ 8

23. What is the least common multiple of 3 and 8?

    Ⓐ 18   Ⓑ 24

    Ⓒ 12   Ⓓ 48

24. Kareem needs 30 hamburger buns for a picnic. The buns come in packages of 8. How many packages should he buy?

    Ⓐ 8   Ⓑ 30

    Ⓒ 4   Ⓓ 10

25. A rectangular rug is about 12 feet long. Its area is about 130 square feet. What is the widest that the rug could be?

    Ⓐ 9 feet   Ⓑ 11 feet

    Ⓒ 13 feet   Ⓓ 18 feet

Practice Test

Choose the correct answer.

26. The refund on a bottle is 5 cents. How many bottles did Jim return to the grocery store if he received 60 cents?

Ⓐ 10　　　Ⓑ 15

Ⓒ 12　　　Ⓓ 20

27. Jill has 20 sweatshirts. She can fit 5 in a box. How many boxes will she need?

Ⓐ 3　　　Ⓑ 4

Ⓒ 5　　　Ⓓ cannot tell

Choose the answer that shows the number in standard form.

28. 90,000 + 800 + 20 + 6

Ⓐ 98,260　Ⓑ 90,806

Ⓒ 90,826　Ⓓ 90,268

29. 400,000 + 30 + 1

Ⓐ 400,031　Ⓑ 400,013

Ⓒ 400,301　Ⓓ 400,103

Solve the following.

30. Round 5,791 to the nearest ten.

Ⓐ 5,800　　Ⓑ 5,790

Ⓒ 5,700　　Ⓓ 5,810

31. Round 361 to the nearest hundred.

Ⓐ 300　　　　　Ⓑ 360

Ⓒ 350　　　　　Ⓓ 400

32.　403
　　－ 15

Ⓐ 388　　　　　Ⓑ 312

Ⓒ 418　　　　　Ⓓ 398

e Textbook This lesson is available in the *eTextbook*.

Extended Response ▶ **Solve** each problem.

33. Rudi's class was playing a review game for social studies. The class was divided into two teams. Rudi's team got 1 point when a question was answered correctly and lost 1 point for an incorrect answer. Find out how many points Rudi's team won looking at the list of answers below:

incorrect, incorrect, correct, correct, correct, incorrect, correct, correct, correct, correct, correct, incorrect.

Ⓐ −4   Ⓑ −3

Ⓒ 3   Ⓓ 4

34. Mrs. Wiles, the librarian, received 9 boxes of new books for the library. The invoice listed a total of 1,450 new books purchased.

a. How many books were in each box?

b. Explain and show how you found your answer. Did every box have the same number of books?

c. If each shelf in the library could fit about 10 more books, how many shelves would be needed to house the new books?

35. Write a word problem that can be solved by using the equation $5 \times n = 20$. What does n equal?

Graphing and Functions

In This Chapter You Will Learn

- how to plot points on a coordinate grid.
- how to use and graph ordered pairs.
- how to graph functions.

Problem Solving

Imagine you are starting your own photography business. You decide to charge $4 for each hour you work.

The bar graph shows how much you will charge for various hours of work.

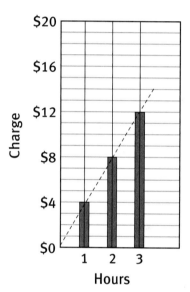

Work in groups to solve these problems. Use the graph or any strategy you like to help you.

1 What pattern do you see in the graph? Why do you think the pattern will or will not continue?

2 If you work from 9:00 A.M. to 3:45 P.M., how much will you charge?

3 How did you solve this problem?

Points on a Grid

Key Ideas

We use points to identify locations on a grid.
Graph City is laid out with numbered streets running north and south, and numbered avenues running east and west.

A place where two (or more) lines cross, such as the streets in Graph City, is called an intersection.

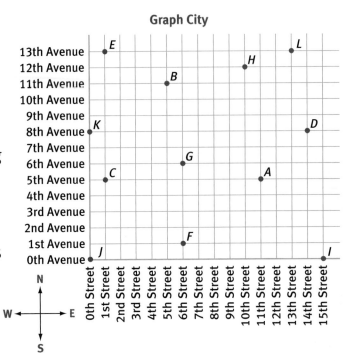

Graph City

Use the map of Graph City to answer these questions.

1. If you went to the corner of 11th Street and 5th Avenue, at which point would you be?

2. Where is point *B*?

3. Suppose a friend in Graph City asked you to meet her at the corner of 11th and 5th. Where would you go?

4. If your friend didn't go to the same place you went, where do you think she might be?

5. **Extended Response** What would you do about it?

e Textbook This lesson is available in the *eTextbook*.

Suppose the people of Graph City agree to always give the street name first and the avenue name second. Knowing that, answer these questions.

6 Where is the corner of 11th and 5th?

7 Where is the corner of 5th and 11th?

8 How many blocks would you have to walk to get from 11th and 5th to 5th and 11th? (Do not cut across blocks.)

9 Is there more than one way to get from 11th and 5th to 5th and 11th by walking only 12 blocks?

10 Suppose you don't cut across blocks and you don't walk in a wrong direction on purpose:
   a. Do all ways of getting from 11th and 5th to 5th and 11th require walking exactly 12 blocks?
   b. What must you do to make the path longer?

11 How many blocks would you have to walk to get from 8th and 8th to 8th and 8th?

12 How many blocks would you have to walk to get from 4th and 7th to 6th and 3rd?

13 **Extended Response** Suppose you live at point *C* and your friend lives at point *D*. Describe the path you would take to get to your friend's house if you were walking.

14 Thomas lives at the corner of 6th Street and 6th Avenue (point *G*). On Sunday, he needs to go to the General Store (point *A*), the rental store (point *C*), and the library (point *B*). Finally, he wants to go to his friend's house (point *F*) before returning home (point *G*). However, Thomas does not want to walk more than 30 blocks total.
   a. Can he visit all of these places without walking at least 30 blocks?
   b. Come up with a route allowing Thomas to visit the most places and return home without going more than 30 blocks.

Give the location of these points on the map of Graph City. Always give the street name first and the avenue name second. The first one has been done for you.

15 A 11th and 5th   16 E   17 I   18 B

19 F   20 J   21 C   22

23 K   24 D   25 H

Key Ideas

Places on a graph can be located quickly by ordered pairs of numbers called coordinates.

In this lesson, you'll learn how to find and name coordinates of locations in Graph City.

You may remember that the people in Graph City say "11th and 5th" as a short way to say "the corner of 11th Street and 5th Avenue."

Here's an even shorter way: (11, 5).

You can use this way to find points on the graph on page 143. For example, to tell where point B is, you can write (3, 8).

How would you tell where point E is?

The coordinates of point E are (13, 2).

The horizontal (sideways) coordinate is given first. The vertical (up-down) coordinate is given second.

Answer these questions using the graph on page 143.

1. What are the coordinates of point D?

2. What are the coordinates of point M?

3. What are the coordinates of point A?

4. What are the coordinates of point X?

5. What are the coordinates of point Z?

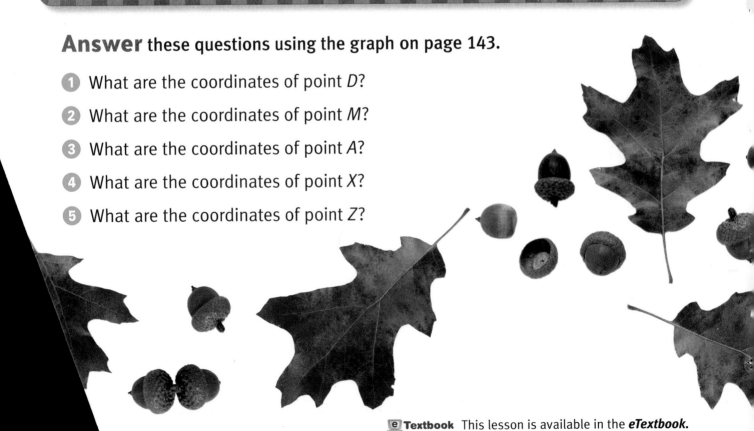

Solve these riddles by writing the correct letter for each of the coordinates from the graph on page 143.

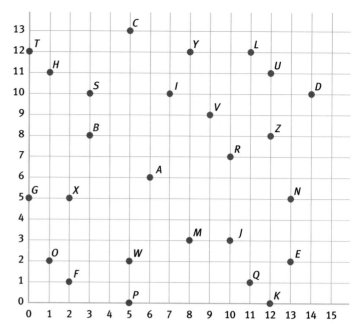

6 What did the acorn say when it grew up?

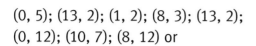

(0, 5); (13, 2); (1, 2); (8, 3); (13, 2); (0, 12); (10, 7); (8, 12) or

▪▪▪ ▪▪ ▪▪ ▪ ▪▪▪▪

(0, 5); (13, 2); (13, 2) (7,10); (8, 3) (6,6); (0,12); (10, 7); (13,2); (13,2)

7 Which president of the United States had a last name that is a homophone of a word that means "a person who makes, alters, or mends clothing"?

▪▪▪▪▪▪

(0, 12); (6, 6); (8, 12); (11, 12); (1, 2); (10, 7)

8 Which two presidents of the United States had the same names as cars?

▪▪▪▪ and ▪▪▪▪▪▪▪

(2, 1); (1, 2); (10, 7); (14, 10) and (11, 12); (7, 10); (13, 5); (5, 13); (1, 2); (11, 12); (13, 5)

9 What kind of sand is found at the bottom of the Pacific Ocean?

▪▪▪ ▪▪▪▪

(5, 2); (13, 2); (0, 12)   (3, 10); (6, 6); (13, 5); (14, 10)

10 List all of the points that are three steps away along straight lines from (5, 4).

| Writing + Math 　**Journal**

Explain why listing pairs of numbers in a standard order, such as listing the street name first and the avenue name second, makes a difference when you are locating points on a grid.

Game

Coordinates and Strategies Practice

Get the Point Game

Players: Two

Materials: Graph paper, crayons or markers (four colors), a black pen or pencil

Object: To find the location of a secret point

Math Focus: Locating and plotting points on a graph, intuitive geometry, and mathematical reasoning; recognizing the fact that order is important when reporting coordinates

HOW TO PLAY

1. Decide what size playing field will be used. Each player then makes his or her own playing field by drawing axis lines on separate sheets of graph paper.

2. The first player chooses a secret point and draws two straight lines through the point. These lines need to be drawn at angles to the axes as shown in the example on the next page so that they cross through other intersections on the grid. This separates the playing field into four parts. The first player colors each of the four parts in a different color.

3. Without seeing what the first player has done, the second player guesses a point by calling out its location using coordinates. Then the first player tells the color of the playing field at that point. A point on one of the two dividing lines is described as black. The second player records this information with the appropriate color on their grid.

4. The second player keeps guessing until he or she finds the secret point.

5. As an option, the player guessing the location of his or her opponent's point in the fewest guesses will be the winner. Students should play the game as often as time permits to see who can find the secret point in the fewest moves.

SAMPLE GAME

Lisa and Max decided on a playing field that goes from 0 to 7 on each axis. Lisa was the first player. She chose (4, 5) as the secret point, drew the two diagonal lines, and colored the sections as shown.

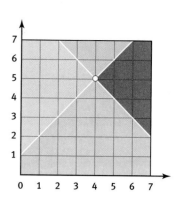

Max made a playing field like Lisa's, but his had no lines or colors. On his field, Max kept a record of each move.

1 Max said, "(6, 5)." Lisa said, "Red." Max circled the point in red.

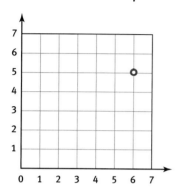

2 Max said, "(5, 2)." Lisa said, "Blue." Max circled that point in blue.

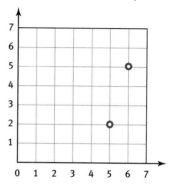

3 Max said, "(5, 4)." Lisa said, "Black." Max knew there was a line there and circled that point in black.

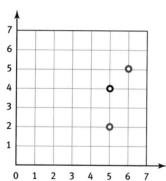

4 Max said, "(3, 3)." Lisa said, "Blue." Max circled that point in blue.

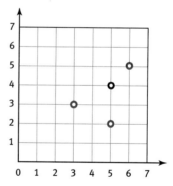

5 Max said, "(2, 4)." Lisa said, "Yellow." Max circled point (2, 4) in yellow. He then knew that there was a line between (3, 3) and (2, 4).

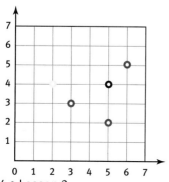

6 Max said, "(4, 5)." Lisa said, "That's the point I chose! You got it in six moves."

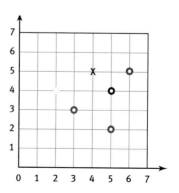

Lengths of Lines on a Grid

Key Ideas

There are a few ways to find the lengths of line segments on a grid.

You can count the units between each point. Another way is to use coordinates.

For example, you can subtract the y-coordinates of points A and B to find the length of AB in the right triangle above.
$7 - 3 = 4$

To find the length of BC, you can subtract the x-coordinates of points B and C.
$6 - 3 = 3$

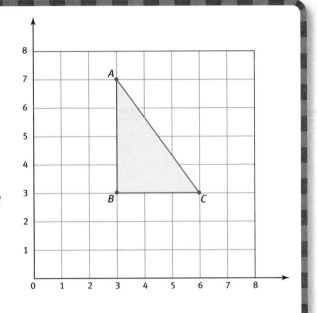

The units on the coordinate grid are 1 centimeter.

1. **Extended Response** How many centimeters is it from A to B? How can you tell?

2. **Extended Response** How many centimeters is it from B to C? How can you tell?

In Lesson 3.4 you learned that the sum of the squares of the lengths of the two shorter sides of a right triangle equals the square of the length of the longest side. This relationship is called the Pythagorean Theorem.

3. **Extended Response** In Triangle ABC, $AB = 4$ cm and $BC = 3$ cm. How long do you think AC is? Why?

4. If you drew a square on side AB, what would be the area of that square?

5. If you drew a square on side BC, what would be the area of that square?

6. According to the Pythagorean Theorem, what would be the area of a square drawn on side AC?

7. What is the length of side AC?

e Textbook This lesson is available in the *eTextbook*.

Draw a 12 × 12 grid on graph paper like the one on page 146. Plot points *D*, *E*, and *F*, using coordinates: *D* (1, 3); *E* (9, 3); and *F* (9, 9). Use your grid to answer the following questions.

8 What is the length of side *DE*?

9 What is the length of side *EF*?

10 What would be the area of a square drawn on side *DE*?

11 What would be the area of a square drawn on side *EF*?

12 Using the Pythagorean Theorem, what would be the area of a square drawn on side *DF*?

13 What is the length of side *DF*?

Draw another 12 × 12 grid on graph paper. Use your grid to answer the following questions.

The coordinates of *R*, *S*, and *T* are *R* (0, 5); *S* (0, 0); and *T* (12, 0).

14 What are the lengths of sides *RS* and *ST*?

15 What is the area of a square with *RS* as its side?

16 What is the area of a square with *ST* as its side?

17 What is the area of a square with *RT* as its side?

18 **Extended Response** What is the length of side *RT*? Explain how you found your answer.

Key Ideas

This function machine performs the same action on all numbers that are put into it.

If you put in a 7, a 12 will come out.

We will write that like this:

7 —⟶(?)⟶ 12

Arrows should be straight. They can go in any direction, but they must point from the number going in to the number coming out.

If we put in 10, 15 will come out.

10 —⟶(?)⟶ 15

This set of arrow operations shows what happens when we put in 0, 4, 9, and 25.

0 —⟶(?)⟶ 5   4 —⟶(?)⟶ 9

9 —⟶(?)⟶ 14   25 —⟶(?)⟶ 30

Each number that comes out is 5 more than the number that went in.

The function rule for this machine is add 5. We will write the add 5 function like this:

—⟶(+ 5)⟶

Find a function rule for each set of arrow operations.

1

3	10
6	13
8	15
1	8

2

3	6
4	8
5	10
1	2

3

4	12
5	15
7	21
0	0

4

8	6
5	3
2	0
3	1

5

10	5
20	15
5	0
6	1

6

8	4
4	2
2	1
0	0

7

9	3
12	4
30	10
3	1

8

5	5
8	8
126	126
3	3

9

3	27
5	45
1	9
8	72

Suppose you put 3 into a function machine and 15 comes out. What could the function rule be?

The function rule could be ×5.

If the function rule was ×5 and 5 went into the machine, 25 would come out.

Let's see what happens when 5 goes into the function machine.

The function rule cannot be ×5.

The function rule +12 works with both examples, since 3 + 12 = 15 and 5 + 12 = 17.

When you try to figure out function rules, it is important to use at least two examples and to be sure that the rule fits both of them.

Write two possible function rules for each of the following function machines.

⑩   4 ⟶ ▢ ⟶ 8   ⑮ 50 ⟶ ▢ ⟶ 10

⑪ 30 ⟶ ▢ ⟶ 15   ⑯ 15 ⟶ ▢ ⟶ 30

⑫ 10 ⟶ ▢ ⟶ 20   ⑰   6 ⟶ ▢ ⟶ 54

⑬ 125 ⟶ ▢ ⟶ 500   ⑱   1 ⟶ ▢ ⟶ 1

⑭   3 ⟶ ▢ ⟶ 21

ⓔ **Textbook** This lesson is available in the *eTextbook*.

The rule for a certain function machine is +4. If you put the number 7 into the machine, what number will come out?

Here's another way to ask the same question.

$$7 \longrightarrow \boxed{+4} \longrightarrow y$$

What is y?

Since $7 + 4 = 11$, y is 11.

Find y. Algebra

19 $16 \longrightarrow \boxed{\div 4} \longrightarrow y$

20 $20 \longrightarrow \boxed{\div 5} \longrightarrow y$

21 $43 \longrightarrow \boxed{-8} \longrightarrow y$

22 $5 \longrightarrow \boxed{+0} \longrightarrow y$

23 $5 \longrightarrow \boxed{-0} \longrightarrow y$

24 $5 \longrightarrow \boxed{\times 1} \longrightarrow y$

25 $5 \longrightarrow \boxed{\div 1} \longrightarrow y$

26 $7 \longrightarrow \boxed{\times 8} \longrightarrow y$

27 $7 \longrightarrow \boxed{\times 0} \longrightarrow y$

28 **Extended Response** Diego, Chaz, and Luna wanted to make fresh orange juice for their family. Their grandfather gave them 21 oranges. Chaz, who went first, made 1 cup of juice from 3 oranges. Diego took 6 oranges and managed to squeeze 2 cups of juice. Luna will squeeze the remaining 12 oranges.
  a. How many cups of fresh orange juice can she hope to make?
  b. How do you know this?
  c. How many total cups of fresh orange juice will Diego, Chaz, and Luna make for their family?

Writing + Math **Journal**
Write a function rule and show four pairs of numbers that could be generated by your rule.

Key Ideas

An inverse function does the opposite of the original function.

Look at this example.

Sarah made $5 each hour she worked at her aunt's house. She was there for 3 hours, so she made a total of $15. This function machine is one way to show what Sarah did.

Look again at the story, and try to find the difference.

Sarah made a total of $15 working at her aunt's house. She worked there for 3 hours. Therefore, she made $5 each hour.

If you put 5 into the first machine, you get out 15. The second machine does the opposite. If you put in 15, you get out 5.

Because these machines do opposite things, we say ___ ×3 → is the inverse of ___ ÷3 → and ___ ÷3 → is the inverse of ___ ×3 →

Tory's puppy weighed 12 pounds when she got him. Since then he has gained 5 pounds.

A function for this would add 5 to the puppy's 12-pound weight.

What would be the inverse for this function?

When starting with +5, the inverse, or opposite, becomes −5.

Write the inverse operation.

1 +7 →

2 ×5 →

3 −12 →

4 ÷4 →

5 Suppose a function machine followed this rule:
What number could you put in to get 21? x ── ×3 ──→ y

Inverse arrow operations can help you find which number went into a machine.

Example: x ── ×6 ──→ 18   What is x?

Use the inverse arrow operations.

x ── ×6 ──→ 18   We know that $18 \div 6 = 3$.

So the value of x is 3.

← ÷6 ──

Use inverse arrow operations, if they help you, to find the value of x.

6 x ── +7 ──→ 8   **7** x ── +17 ──→ 19   **8** x ── −3 ──→ 10

9 x ── ×5 ──→ 25   **10** x ── ×10 ──→ 90   **11** x ── ÷4 ──→ 8

12 x ── −15 ──→ 0   **13** x ── ×0 ──→ 0   **14** x ── ÷7 ──→ 2

15 x ── +86 ──→ 100   **16** x ── ×2 ──→ 100   **17** x ── ÷10 ──→ 4

18 x ── ×8 ──→ 8   **19** x ── ×10 ──→ 100   **20** x ── +99 ──→ 100

21 x ── +0 ──→ 0   **22** x ── −8 ──→ 11   **23** x ── ×5 ──→ 35

24 **Extended Response** For Problem 13, can x have more than one value? Explain your answer.

Key Ideas

We can use ordered pairs to identify points on a grid.
An ordered pair is made by naming the x-coordinate first and then the y-coordinate.

Look at this function machine.

It works according to this rule:

$$x \longrightarrow (+5) \longrightarrow y$$

If you put in 7, then 12 comes out.

$$7 \longrightarrow (+5) \longrightarrow 12$$

Let's write that pair of numbers like this: (7, 12)

The first number in the pair (7) is the one that went in. The second number in the pair (12) is the one that came out.

A pair of numbers written this way (7, 12) is called an ordered pair. We call it that because the order shows which is the input (7) and which is the output (12).

We can list other ordered pairs for the $+5$ function machine.

If we put in 3, then 8 comes out: (3, 8)

If we put in 9, then 14 comes out: (9, 14)

Textbook This lesson is available in the **eTextbook.**

Copy each list of ordered pairs, but replace the *x* or *y* with
the correct number.

1 *x* ⟶ (+5) ⟶ *y*   (7, 12); (12, *y*); (15, *y*); (0, *y*); (*x*, 7)

2 *x* ⟶ (÷4) ⟶ *y*   (8, 2); (*x*, 4); (*x*, 3); (*x*, 7); (*x*, 9)

3 *x* ⟶ (−3) ⟶ *y*   (9, 6); (7, *y*); (*x*, 7); (12, *y*); (*x*, 1)

4 *x* ⟶ (+8) ⟶ *y*   (5, 13); (4, *y*); (*x*, 11); (*x*, 15); (6, *y*)

5 *x* ⟶ (×5) ⟶ *y*   (1, 5); (3, *y*); (*x*, 10); (0, *y*); (8, *y*)

6 *x* ⟶ (−9) ⟶ *y*   (11, *y*); (20, *y*); (25, *y*); (*x*, 0); (*x*, 8); (*x*, 9)

7 *x* ⟶ (×3) ⟶ *y*   (2, *y*); (4, *y*); (8, *y*); (10, *y*); (*x*, 6); (*x*, 15)

8 *x* ⟶ (÷2) ⟶ *y*   (6, *y*); (18, *y*); (12, *y*); (6, *y*); (*x*, 7); (*x*, 1)

9 *x* ⟶ (×0) ⟶ *y*   (7, *y*); (12, *y*); (50, *y*); (2,589, *y*); (*x*, 0)

10 Morgan is playing 9 holes of golf with her father. On the even-
numbered holes she scored a 6, while on the odd-numbered
holes she scored a 7. Her father scored a total of 46 on all
9 holes. After what hole did Morgan reach her father's score?

11 **Extended Response** Suppose Problem 9 included the ordered pair
(*x*, 7). What would your answer be?

Use function rules to solve the riddles. Find the value of x or y in each ordered pair. Then use the secret code to find what letter each value stands for.

A	B	C	D	E	F	G	H	I	J	K	L	M
26	25	24	23	22	21	20	19	18	17	16	15	14

N	O	P	Q	R	S	T	U	V	W	X	Y	Z
13	12	11	10	9	8	7	6	5	4	3	2	1

12 What is a noisy group of people?

Use this function rule: x ── (+3) ──▶ y

(23, ⬜) (12, ⬜); (⬜, 15); (3, ⬜); (20, ⬜); (21, ⬜);
(6, ⬜); (9, ⬜); (⬜, 7); (⬜, 26)

13 What's another name for a police chief?

Use this function rule: x ── (−5) ──▶ y

(31, ⬜)   (12, ⬜); (17, ⬜); (⬜, 6)   (⬜, 19); (⬜, 7); (16, ⬜)

In each exercise, two of the answers are clearly wrong, and one is correct. Choose the correct answer.

14
$$409$$
$$+\ 618$$
a. 1297
b. 917
c. 1027

15
$$597$$
$$-\ 522$$
a. 25
b. 105
c. 75

16
$$4195$$
$$-\ 3167$$
a. 128
b. 1028
c. 2078

17
$$1618$$
$$+\ 9322$$
a. 15940
b. 12040
c. 10940

e Textbook This lesson is available in the *eTextbook*.

Game

Function Game

Players: Two or more

Materials: Number Cubes: two 0–5 (red), two 5–10 (blue)

Object: To score closest to 100 without going over

Math Focus: Mental math (with all four operations) and mathematical reasoning

HOW TO PLAY

1 Make a blank function machine chart. Use the charts below as a model.

2 The first player rolls all four **Number Cubes** to get the values of x. Write all four values of x in your chart.

3 Select a function, and write it in the blank circle at the top of your chart.

4 Using your function rule, find the values of y.

5 Find the sum of all the values of y.

6 The player with the sum closest to, but not greater than, 100 wins the round.

$$x \longrightarrow \boxed{?} \longrightarrow y$$

SAMPLE GAME

Marc's Chart

$$x \longrightarrow \times 4 \longrightarrow y$$

x	y
5	20
4	16
6	24
8	32

Sum 92

Janel's Chart

$$x \longrightarrow +18 \longrightarrow y$$

x	y
5	23
4	22
6	24
8	26

Sum 95

Malia's Chart

$$x \longrightarrow +20 \longrightarrow y$$

x	y
5	25
4	24
6	26
8	28

Sum 103

Janel was the winner of this round.

Function Rules and Ordered Pairs

Key Ideas

If we are given a function rule, we can make a set of ordered pairs.

If we know: $x \longrightarrow \boxed{-6} \longrightarrow y$ we can find ordered pairs,

such as (8, 2); (12, 6); and (15, 9). Often we can find a

function rule if we are given a set of ordered pairs.

If we know: (8, 2); (12, 6); (15, 9) $x \longrightarrow \boxed{?} \longrightarrow y$

We can determine that the function rule is -6.

Find the values of *x* in the ordered pairs.

1 $x \longrightarrow \boxed{+5} \longrightarrow y$ (*x*, 5); (*x*, 7); (*x*, 15); (*x*, 205); (*x*, 73)

2 $x \longrightarrow \boxed{-5} \longrightarrow y$ (*x*, 5); (*x*, 25); (*x*, 30); (*x*, 35); (*x*, 45)

3 $x \longrightarrow \boxed{\div 8} \longrightarrow y$ (*x*, 1); (*x*, 3); (*x*, 8); (*x*, 9); (*x*, 10)

Copy and complete these charts. Solve for *x* or *y*.

4 $x \longrightarrow \boxed{\times 4} \longrightarrow y$

x	y
1	4
▨	8
6	▨
▨	12
10	▨

5 $x \longrightarrow \boxed{+3} \longrightarrow y$

x	y
▨	7
2	▨
5	▨
▨	25
6	▨

6 $x \longrightarrow \boxed{\times 8} \longrightarrow y$

x	y
0	▨
▨	24
2	▨
1	8
▨	32

ⓔTextbook This lesson is available in the *eTextbook*.

7 $x \xrightarrow{+7} y$

x	y
8	
30	
	27
6	
	107

8 $x \xrightarrow{\times 6} y$

x	y
3	
	54
10	
	48
7	

9 $x \xrightarrow{-3} y$

x	y
	5
	10
	9
24	
3	

10 $x \xrightarrow{\times 7} y$

x	y
7	
0	
10	
	14
	21

11 $x \xrightarrow{-4} y$

x	y
	15
	21
	72
	3
	19

12 $x \xrightarrow{+6} y$

x	y
	25
	35
	45
	55
	65

Find the most likely function rules, then complete these charts.

13 $x \xrightarrow{\square} y$

x	y
3	3
25	25
100	
	7
2	

14 $x \xrightarrow{\square} y$

x	y
3	9
20	60
5	15
	27
	30

15 $x \xrightarrow{\square} y$

x	y
6	0
5	0
20	
31	
12	

Graphing Ordered Pairs

Key Ideas

Once you have used a function rule to find ordered pairs, you can use the ordered pairs as coordinates to make points on a graph to visualize the function.

Janice recorded the number of baskets she made during her last 6 basketball games. She now wants to find out how many points she scored and graph her progress.

Janice's coordinates are:

(1, 2); (2, 4); (3, 6); (4, 8); (5, 10); (6, 12)

To make a line on a graph, at least two points are needed. *Any* ordered pair following a specific function rule will be placed on the same line. If Janice's ordered pairs are placed on a grid, you will notice a line. Functions that create straight lines when graphed are referred to as linear functions.

$x \rightarrow \boxed{\times 2} \rightarrow y$

x	y
1	?
2	?
3	?
4	?
5	?
6	?

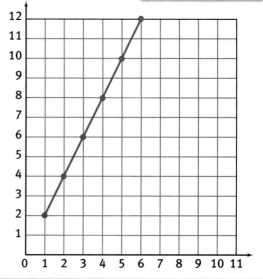

Complete the following problems.

1. Copy the list of ordered pairs, but replace each *x* or *y* with the correct number.

   $x \rightarrow \boxed{+2} \rightarrow y$ (−2, y); (−4, y); (3, y); (x, −3); (x, 4); (x, 7)

2. Make a graph using the ordered pairs you found in Problem 1.

3. What do you notice about the six points on your graph?

Note: Remember the first number (*x*) tells how far to go to the right or left. The second number (*y*) tells how far to go up.

e Textbook This lesson is available in the *eTextbook*.

Look at your graph, but don't do any calculations for Problems 4 and 5.

④ Think about the point on the line that has 4 as its first coordinate.
  a. Where do you think the point should be?
  b. What is its second coordinate?
  c. If 4 were put into a +2 function machine, what would come out?

⑤ Copy each ordered pair, but replace each *x* or *y* with the number you believe would make the point fall on the line.

  a. $(-1, y)$ **b.** $(x, 2)$ **c.** $(x, 8)$ **d.** $(1, y)$

Copy each list of ordered pairs, but replace each *x* or *y* with the correct number. Then graph each set of ordered pairs to see the slope of the line.

⑥ *x* ——(−3)——▸ *y* $(5, y)$; $(1, y)$; $(4, y)$; $(x, 2)$; $(x, 5)$; $(0, y)$

⑦ *x* ——(÷2)——▸ *y* $(4, y)$; $(6, y)$; $(20, y)$; $(x, 4)$; $(x, 8)$; $(10, y)$

⑧ *x* ——(×2)——▸ *y* $(1, y)$; $(3, y)$; $(0, y)$; $(10, y)$; $(5, y)$; $(9, y)$

⑨ *x* ——(+0)——▸ *y* $(1, y)$; $(3, y)$; $(0, y)$; $(x, 9)$; $(x, 12)$; $(x, 8)$

⑩ *x* ——(×1)——▸ *y* $(1, y)$; $(3, y)$; $(0, y)$; $(x, 9)$; $(x, 12)$; $(x, 8)$

Juan is using his new camera to make an album about Graph City. After he took a photo of an elm tree this morning, he walked in a zigzag path, as shown on the list to the right, snapping pictures as he went. He ended up at 23rd Street and 16th Avenue. He wants to go back and photograph the elm tree again.

Where is the elm tree?

Juan's Path

3 blocks north

2 blocks east

2 blocks north

5 blocks east

1 block south

2 blocks east

Kim solved the problem this way:

I started to solve the problem by Making a Diagram and Working Backward.

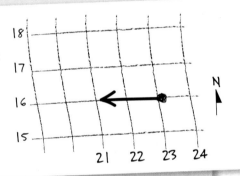

Juan ended up at 23rd and 16th.

Before that he walked 2 blocks east.

That means he was at 21st and 16th.

Before that he walked 1 block south.

That means he was at. . .

Think about Kim's strategy. Answer these questions.

1. Why did Kim draw an arrow going 2 blocks west to find out where Juan was before he walked 2 blocks east?

2. What will Kim draw next to show where Juan was before he walked 1 block south?

3. Where was Juan just before he walked 1 block south?

4. Can Kim continue to work backward to solve the problem? Explain.

5. Would you use Kim's strategy or a different strategy to solve the problem?

Sonya tried a different strategy.

I made a Table to combine all the times Juan walked east and another table for all the times he walked north and south. Then I planned to Work Backward.

Juan walked east 3 times
2 blocks east
5 blocks east
2 blocks east

Result: 9 blocks east

Juan walked north or south 3 times
3 blocks north
2 blocks north
1 block south

Result: 6 blocks north

The result of all Juan's moves is the same as walking 9 blocks east and 6 blocks north. I can reverse that to find where he started.

Think about Sonya's strategy. Answer these questions.

6 Do you agree that the 3 times Juan walked east had the same result as walking 9 blocks east? Why or why not?

7 Do you agree that the 3 times Juan walked north and south were the same as walking 6 blocks north? Why or why not?

8 Do you think Sonya's strategy could solve the problem? Explain.

9 Which strategy do you prefer, Kim's or Sonya's? Why?

10 Use Kim's strategy, Sonya's strategy, or a strategy of your own to solve the problem. What strategy did you use? How did you check your answer?

Cumulative Review

Relation Signs Lesson 2.4 and 3.10

What is the correct sign? Write <, >, or =.

1. $28 \div 7$ ▨ $48 \div 12$

2. $3 \times 5 + 6$ ▨ 6×4

3. $4 + 4 + 4 + 4$ ▨ $-5 + 20$

4. $9 + 6 \times 0$ ▨ $9 + 6 + 0$

Division with Remainders Lesson 3.11

Divide. Watch for remainders.

5. $10\overline{)85}$
6. $6\overline{)30}$
7. $3\overline{)14}$
8. $5\overline{)40}$
9. $9\overline{)62}$

Multidigit Addition and Subtraction Lesson 2.3

Compute the following.

10. $365 + 423 =$ ▨

11. $9,000 - 654 =$ ▨

12. $736 - 252 =$ ▨

13. $45,673 + 98,609 =$ ▨

14. $32,020 - 5,492 =$ ▨

Perimeter Lesson 1.8

Solve.

15. A tennis court is 36 feet wide and 78 feet long. What is the perimeter of the court?

16. The Conlan family installed a rectangular swimming pool.

   a. Find the area of the pool if it was 8 meters long and 6 meters wide.

   b. Is the area of this pool larger or smaller than the area of a pool that is 7 meters long and 7 meters wide?

Cumulative Review

Parentheses **Lesson 3.13**

Solve for n. Watch the signs.

17 $27 \div (9 \div 3) = n$ **18** $11 - (4 \times 2) = n$ **19** $(6 \times 5) + (21 \div 3) = n$

20 $(32 \div 8) \times (10 \quad 6) = n$ **21** $(3 \times 6) \div 2 = n$

Applying Math **Lesson 3.14**

Solve each problem.

22 Erica bought 8 pencils. They cost 9¢ each. She gave the storekeeper 75¢. How much change should she get?

23 About what is the length of a string that is made by tying two 9-meter strings together?

24 William paid 48¢ for 6 carrots. How much did each carrot cost?

25 Vance has 47 pears. He wants to give an equal number of pears to each of 4 children, but he also wants to keep at least 10 pears for himself.

a. How many pears should he give to each child?

b. How many pears should he keep for himself?

Common Multiples and Common Factors **Lesson 3.12**

Find two common multiples for each set of numbers.

26 3 and 4   **27** 8 and 9   **28** 4 and 7   **29** 8 and 3   **30** 12 and 5

Ⓔ **Textbook** This lesson is available in the **eTextbook.**

Key Ideas Review

In this chapter you calculated functions to build and interpret graphs.

You learned what a function is and how it works.

You learned how to read graphs.

Use the grid to solve the exercises below.

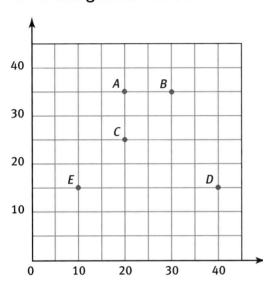

1. What are the coordinates of point *B*?

2. What are the coordinates of point *D*?

3. **Extended Response** Explain how to plot an ordered pair on a grid.

Fill in the blanks for the following functions

4. ▢ ——(−3)——▶ 9

5. 24 ——(÷4)——▶ ▢

6. 12 ——(×3)——▶ ? ——(÷6)——▶ ▢

7. x —▢—▶ y

x	y
28	7
36	9
44	11
8	2

8. x —+15—▶ y

x	y
10	▢
20	▢
30	▢
40	▢

Lessons 4.1 and 4.2 **Name** the coordinates of the points on the graph.

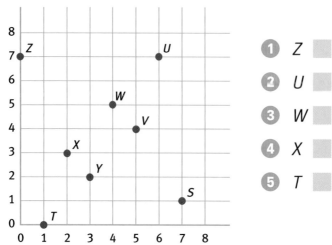

1. Z ▨
2. U ▨
3. W ▨
4. X ▨
5. T ▨

Lesson 4.5 **Find** the value of *x* or *y*.

6. $x \longrightarrow \boxed{+2} \longrightarrow 8$ $x = $ ▨

7. $4 \longrightarrow \boxed{\times 2} \longrightarrow y$ $y = $ ▨

8. $x \longrightarrow \boxed{\times 5} \longrightarrow 20$ $x = $ ▨

Lesson 4.4 **Find** a function rule.

9.

$x \longrightarrow \bigcirc \longrightarrow y$

x	y
5	8
7	10
11	14
9	12

10.

$x \longrightarrow \bigcirc \longrightarrow y$

x	y
3	12
5	20
9	36
6	24

e Textbook This lesson is available in the *eTextbook*.

Answer the following questions.

11 The corners of Triangle *ABC* are at *A* (2, 2), *B* (6, 2) and *C* (6, 5). What is the length of *AC*?

12 Felipe bought 6 pairs of socks. Each pair cost $3, including tax. He gave the clerk $20. How much change should he receive?

Lessons 4.1, 4.7, and 4.8

Complete these tables. Then graph each set of ordered pairs. Make sure your graph will fit on your paper.

13 $x \to \times 3 \to y$

x	y
	18
	27
5	
	12

14 $x \to \div 4 \to y$

x	y
28	
12	
	5
16	4

15 $x \to +10 \to y$

x	y
25	
	15
7	
16	

16 $x \to +7 \to y$

x	y
0	
3	
	15
	20

17 $x \to -3 \to y$

x	y
3	
	6
	8
13	

Look at the graph. Find the coordinates of the following points.

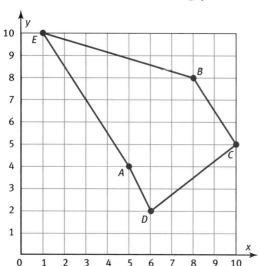

1. point A

   Ⓐ (4, 5)   Ⓑ (5, 4)

   Ⓒ (6, 2)   Ⓓ None of the above

2. point B

   Ⓐ (7, 5)   Ⓑ (6, 4)

   Ⓒ (4, 7)   Ⓓ None of the above

3. point C

   Ⓐ (10, 5)   Ⓑ (5, 4)

   Ⓒ (1, 3)   Ⓓ (6, 2)

4. point D

   Ⓐ (6, 4)   Ⓑ (5, 4)

   Ⓒ (6, 2)   Ⓓ None of the above

5. point E

   Ⓐ (10, 1)   Ⓑ (8, 2)

   Ⓒ (1, 10)   Ⓓ None of the above

Find the value of x or y.

6. $5 \longrightarrow \boxed{+5} \longrightarrow y$

   Ⓐ 0   Ⓑ 11

   Ⓒ 10   Ⓓ None of the above

7. $8 \longrightarrow \boxed{-3} \longrightarrow y$

   Ⓐ 6   Ⓑ 11

   Ⓒ 2   Ⓓ None of the above

8. $x \longrightarrow \boxed{+6} \longrightarrow 15$

   Ⓐ 9   Ⓑ 3

   Ⓒ 10   Ⓓ 8

9. $x \longrightarrow \boxed{\times 8} \longrightarrow 48$

   Ⓐ 6   Ⓑ 9

   Ⓒ 3   Ⓓ 8

10. $x \longrightarrow \boxed{-4} \longrightarrow 3$

    Ⓐ 9   Ⓑ 7

    Ⓒ 8   Ⓓ None of the above

11. $5 \longrightarrow \boxed{+5} \longrightarrow y$

    Ⓐ 6   Ⓑ 11

    Ⓒ 10   Ⓓ 0

ⓔ Textbook This lesson is available in the **eTextbook.**

Solve the following.

12. The refund on a pop bottle is 5 cents. How many bottles did Jim return to the grocery store if he received 60 cents?

    Ⓐ 10   Ⓑ 15

    Ⓒ 12   Ⓓ 20

13. Jill has 20 sweatshirts. She can fit 5 in a box. How many boxes will she need?

    Ⓐ 3   Ⓑ 4

    Ⓒ 5   Ⓓ cannot tell

14. Kareem needs 30 hamburger buns for a picnic. Buns come in packages of 8. How many packages should he buy?

    Ⓐ 8   Ⓑ 30

    Ⓒ 4   Ⓓ 10

15. Ron bought 11 pencils. Each pencil costs 7 cents. He gave the cashier 80¢. How much change should he get?

    Ⓐ 3¢   Ⓑ 10¢

    Ⓒ 2¢   Ⓓ 15¢

16. About what length is a strip of fabric made by stitching together three 8-foot strips?

    Ⓐ a little more than 24 feet

    Ⓑ a little more than 20 feet

    Ⓒ a little less than 24 feet

    Ⓓ a little less than 20 feet

17. A rectangular rug is about 12 feet long. Its area is less than 130 square feet. What is the widest that the rug could be?

    Ⓐ 9 feet   Ⓑ 11 feet

    Ⓒ 13 feet   Ⓓ 18 feet

18. Katie has 40 oranges to share among 8 people. How many will each receive?

    Ⓐ 5   Ⓑ 8

    Ⓒ 4   Ⓓ 6

19. Jamie has 80 grapes. He wants to give an equal number of grapes to each of 5 friends. He wants to keep at least 15 for himself. How many can he give to each friend?

    Ⓐ 15   Ⓑ 13

    Ⓒ 17   Ⓓ 19

20. Which of the following numbers is a common factor of 56 and 63?

Ⓐ 6 Ⓑ 7

Ⓒ 8 Ⓓ 9

21. A large classroom will hold 108 chairs. How should the teacher and her students arrange the chairs so that they have equal rows?

Ⓐ 12 rows of 8

Ⓑ 9 rows of 12

Ⓒ 10 rows of 18

Ⓓ 13 rows of 8

22. Which of the following numbers is a common factor of 16 and 24?

Ⓐ 5 Ⓑ 10

Ⓒ 8 Ⓓ 6

23. Peggy's swimming pool is between 9 and 10 meters long and between 8 and 9 meters wide. What is the least area the pool can be?

Ⓐ 72 m^2 Ⓑ 80 m^2

Ⓒ 81 m^2 Ⓓ 75 m^2

24. What is the greatest area the pool can be?

Ⓐ 80 m^2 Ⓑ 81 m^2

Ⓒ 90 m^2 Ⓓ 100 m^2

Solve the following exercises about functions and graphs.

25. Jaclyn makes bracelets to sell at school. She buys more supplies with the money she makes from selling bracelets. She makes a 7¢ profit on each bracelet. Which function rule relates Jaclyn's profit to the number of bracelets sold?

Ⓐ ×7 Ⓑ −7

Ⓒ +7 Ⓓ ÷7

26. Use the function rule from Problem 25 to compute the ordered pairs.

x	y
10	☐
9	☐
8	☐
7	☐
3	☐
2	☐

27. **Extended Response** On graph paper, graph the ordered pairs showing Jaclyn's profits.

28. Explain why you selected the scale you did.

ⓔ Textbook This lesson is available in the *eTextbook.*

Extended Response ▶ **Solve** the following.

29. Ms. Terrell needs 54 tiles for a new kitchen floor.

  a. The tiles come in boxes of
  8 tiles each. It is not possible to buy part of a box.
  How many boxes of tiles will Ms. Terrell need to buy
  to have enough to cover the floor? Show or explain
  how you got your answer.

  b. One box of tiles costs 12 dollars. Ms. Terrell only has
  $100 to spend on tile. Will she have enough money
  to finish the floor? Explain how you found your
  answer.

30. Four friends wanted to share 3 different pizzas.

  a. If the pizzas were cut into 8 slices each, how many
  slices would each friend get? Would there be any
  pizza left over? Explain.

  b. If the pizzas were cut into 10 slices, how many slices
  would each friend get? Would there be any pizza left
  over? Explain.

In This Chapter You Will Learn

- how to multiply by powers of 10.
- how to convert metric units.
- how to multiply two- and three-digit numbers by one-digit numbers.

Problem Solving

Have you ever felt your heart beating fast when you were playing a sport or racing on your bike? What happened to your heartbeat afterward?

These graphs show the heart rate of two athletes who are playing a sport. Can you figure out which sport?

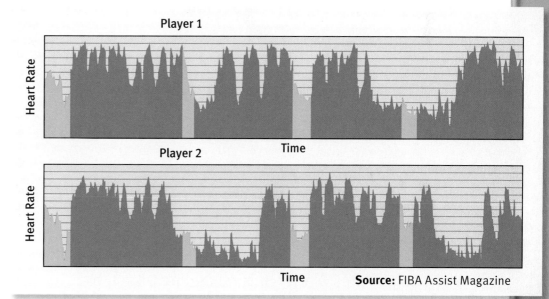

Source: FIBA Assist Magazine

Work in groups. Copy the chart and list different sports these athletes could be playing. For each sport, discuss why you think the athletes were playing that sport or why you think they were not. Record your reasons.

Sport	Reasons For or Against

Malik said, "If I had found the 28 first, we wouldn't have to write so much. I could write the 8 and then add the 2 tens to the 14 tens without writing the 28 at all!"

$$\begin{array}{r} 24 \\ \times\ 7 \\ \hline 8 \end{array}$$
Start at the right because it is easier. Multiply the ones digit by 7.

$7 \times 4 = 28$ (28 is 2 tens and 8 ones)

Write the 8 and **remember the 2 tens** for the next column.

$$\begin{array}{r} 24 \\ \times\ 7 \\ \hline 168 \end{array}$$
Multiply the tens digit by 7.

$7 \times 2 = 14$

The 14 tens **plus the 2 tens you remembered** is 16 tens. Write 16.

· ·

You may have trouble remembering the number that you saved from the previous column. If you do, you may use one of these methods to help:

a. Keep track of the number on your fingers. If the number is greater than 5, use both hands; you won't have to write until you've used that number.

b. You may write the number you are remembering in the place you will write the next part of the answer. Cross off the number as soon as you use it.

$$\begin{array}{r} 24 \\ \times\ 7 \\ \hline \end{array} \longrightarrow \begin{array}{r} 24 \\ \times\ 7 \\ \hline {}^{2}\ 8 \end{array} \longrightarrow \begin{array}{r} 24 \\ \times\ 7 \\ \hline \cancel{1}68 \end{array}$$

c. Write the number above the next digit of the top number. Cross it off when you use it.

$$\begin{array}{r} 24 \\ \times\ 7 \\ \hline \end{array} \longrightarrow \begin{array}{r} {}^{2} \\ 24 \\ \times\ 7 \\ \hline 8 \end{array} \longrightarrow \begin{array}{r} \cancel{2} \\ 24 \\ \times\ 7 \\ \hline 168 \end{array}$$

If you write the numbers, be sure to make them small and neat so you don't get confused.

Multiply. Use shortcuts when you can. Check to see that your answers make sense.

1
$$\begin{array}{r} 24 \\ \times\ 6 \\ \hline \end{array}$$

2
$$\begin{array}{r} 26 \\ \times\ 9 \\ \hline \end{array}$$

3
$$\begin{array}{r} 43 \\ \times\ 3 \\ \hline \end{array}$$

4
$$\begin{array}{r} 3 \\ \times\ 43 \\ \hline \end{array}$$

5
$$\begin{array}{r} 60 \\ \times\ 8 \\ \hline \end{array}$$

6
$$\begin{array}{r} 90 \\ \times\ 3 \\ \hline \end{array}$$

7
$$\begin{array}{r} 89 \\ \times\ 3 \\ \hline \end{array}$$

8
$$\begin{array}{r} 24 \\ \times\ 8 \\ \hline \end{array}$$

9
$$\begin{array}{r} 28 \\ \times\ 4 \\ \hline \end{array}$$

10
$$\begin{array}{r} 46 \\ \times\ 7 \\ \hline \end{array}$$

11
$$\begin{array}{r} 19 \\ \times\ 4 \\ \hline \end{array}$$

12
$$\begin{array}{r} 78 \\ \times\ 9 \\ \hline \end{array}$$

13
$$\begin{array}{r} 57 \\ \times\ 7 \\ \hline \end{array}$$

14
$$\begin{array}{r} 25 \\ \times\ 4 \\ \hline \end{array}$$

15
$$\begin{array}{r} 87 \\ \times\ 2 \\ \hline \end{array}$$

16
$$\begin{array}{r} 51 \\ \times\ 7 \\ \hline \end{array}$$

17 $68 \times 3 =$

18 $26 \times 9 =$

19 $6 \times 39 =$

20 $72 \times 8 =$

21 $37 \times 5 =$

22 $7 \times 49 =$

23 $68 \times 5 =$

24 $29 \times 3 =$

25 $99 \times 8 =$

26 $91 \times 2 =$

27 $85 \times 4 =$

28 $77 \times 8 =$

29 $40 \times 3 =$

30 $4 \times 72 =$

31 $6 \times 58 =$

32 **Extended Response** How do you know that 378 is not the correct answer for Problem 31?

Solve these problems.

33 Reuben wants to plant a flower garden. He is thinking about having 4 rows of plants. He figures that he can plant 16 plants per row.

    a. Using this plan, how many flowers could he plant in his garden?

    b. If Reuben decides to add one more row of plants, how many flowers would he have?

34 After planting his flower garden, Reuben wants to apply some mulch to protect the garden from weeds. The lawn and garden store sells mulch in two sizes: 48-pound bags and 24-pound bags.

    a. If Reuben buys 3 of the 48-pound bags of mulch, how many pounds of mulch would he have?

    b. If Reuben buys 5 of the 24-pound bags, how much mulch would he have?

35 After a few weeks, Reuben's garden sprouted 8 sunflowers. If each sunflower had 34 petals, how many petals could Reuben see in total?

 **Journal**

Which was the easiest of the last ten questions? Explain why.

Multiplication: Three-Digit by One-Digit

Key Ideas

Multiplying a three-digit number by a one-digit number can be done the same way as multiplying a two-digit number by a one-digit number.

Remember that Adam, Malik, Darryl, and Devon had 168 flowers.

"The school will make 9 cents for each flower we sell," said Adam. "I wonder how much money we can make altogether."

"Let's see," Darryl said, "168 is the same amount as 100 + 60 + 8. For 100 flowers we'll make 900 cents. For 60 flowers we'll make 540 cents. For 8 flowers we'll make 72 cents. How much is that altogether?"

"That's 1,512 cents," said Devon, "which is $15.12."

"Let's go sell some flowers!" they all said.

Look:

$$
\begin{array}{r}
168 \\
\times\ 9 \\
\hline
72 \\
+\ 540 \\
+\ 900 \\
\hline
1512
\end{array}
$$

72 ← This 72 comes from 9 × 8.

540 ← This 540 comes from 9 × 60 (or 9 × 6 tens).

900 ← This 900 comes from 9 × 100 (or 9 × 1 hundred).

1512 ← This 1,512 comes from 72 + 540 + 900.

eTextbook This lesson is available in the *eTextbook*.

Here's a shorter way to multiply 9 × 168.

$$\begin{array}{r} 168 \\ \times\ \ 9 \\ \hline 2 \end{array}$$

Start at the right. Multiply the ones digit by 9.
$9 \times 8 = 72$
$72 = 7$ tens and 2 ones
Write the 2 and remember the 7 tens.

$$\begin{array}{r} 168 \\ \times\ \ 9 \\ \hline 12 \end{array}$$

Multiply the tens digit by 9.
$9 \times 6 = 54$
54 tens and 7 (remembered) tens is 61 tens.
61 tens = 6 hundreds and 1 ten
Write the 1 and remember the 6 hundreds.

$$\begin{array}{r} 168 \\ \times\ \ 9 \\ \hline 1512 \end{array}$$

Multiply the hundreds digit by 9.
$9 \times 1 = 9$
9 hundreds and 6 (remembered) hundreds is 15 hundreds.
15 hundreds is 1 thousand and 5 hundreds.
Write the 15.

Multiply. Use shortcuts when you can. Approximate to check to see if your answers make sense.

1. $352 \times 8 = $ ▢
2. $643 \times 8 = $ ▢
3. $721 \times 2 = $ ▢
4. $684 \times 7 = $ ▢
5. $7 \times 684 = $ ▢
6. $685 \times 7 = $ ▢
7. $47 \times 6 = $ ▢
8. $453 \times 4 = $ ▢
9. $800 \times 6 = $ ▢
10. $308 \times 10 = $ ▢
11. $795 \times 5 = $ ▢
12. $5 \times 796 = $ ▢
13. $200 \times 9 = $ ▢
14. $497 \times 2 = $ ▢
15. $7 \times 607 = $ ▢

Writing + Math **Journal**

Explain the process of multiplying a one-digit number by a three-digit number.

Multiplication Review

Key Ideas

Multiplying multidigit numbers by a one-digit number can be useful in various situations.

Neil received $158 for graduating from high school. Before leaving for college he wants to invest his money in a cell phone. Below is a list of the plans he can choose from.

Plan #1	Plan #2	Plan #3	Plan #4
$10 per month	$20 per month	$25 per month	$30 per month
50 minutes per month	120 minutes per month	180 minutes per month	240 minutes per month
Phone is $30	Phone is $10	Free phone	Free phone

Each plan requires a six-month contract. If Neil can not pay the monthly expenses of the phone, it will be disconnected and he will have to pay a fine.

For Plans 1 and 2 Neil is required to buy the phone, along with his monthly expenses.

Each cell phone plan has strengths and weaknesses. Which of these plans can Neil afford?

e Textbook This lesson is available in the *eTextbook.*

Neil begins by calculating the cost of Plan 1:

The service is $10 a month, and the contract is 6 months.

$10 \times 6 = 60$

The service for this plan will cost $60, plus he needs to buy the phone which is an additional $30.

$60 + $30 = $90   He can afford this plan.

He then looked at Plan 2:

The service was $20 for 6 months.

$20 \times 6 = 120$

The service for this plan will cost $120, plus he needs to pay $10 for a phone.

$120 + $10 = $130   He can afford this plan.

He then looked at Plan 3:

The service was $25 for 6 months.

$25 \times 6 = 150$

The service for this plan will cost $150; however, the phone is free. He can afford this plan.

Plan 4 is $5 more each month than Plan 3, which Neil can just afford. Neil won't have enough to cover the $5 extra for 6 months. So Neil cannot afford Plan 4.

Multiply.

1 64
   × 7
   ▩

2 308
   × 4
   ▩

3 900
   × 9
   ▩

4 726
   × 8
   ▩

5 38
   × 4
   ▩

6 501
   × 8
   ▩

7   2
   × 394
   ▩

8 48
   × 3
   ▩

9 90
   × 9
   ▩

10 307
    × 9
    ▩

11 56 × 7 = ▩

12 321 × 4 = ▩

13 322 × 4 = ▩

14 872 × 7 = ▩

15 82 × 5 = ▩

16 49 × 4 = ▩

17 72 × 6 = ▩

18 19 × 8 = ▩

19 198 × 1 = ▩

20 9 × 840 = ▩

21 28 × 6 = ▩

22 2 × 917 = ▩

23 107 × 5 = ▩

24 730 × 4 = ▩

25 5 × 489 = ▩

ⓔTextbook This lesson is available in the *eTextbook.*

Solve these problems.

26) Jamie rides her bike 3 kilometers every day. How far does she ride in 2 weeks?

27) Judy gets 24 ride tickets in every ticket book she buys. How many ride tickets will she get in 6 books?

28) Antonio is packing supplies for a camping trip. He will bake biscuits 5 times. He will use 4 packages of biscuit mix each time he bakes biscuits. How many packages of biscuit mix should he pack?

29) **Extended Response** Allison works 15 hours a week at the movie rental store. If she makes $5 per hour, how many weeks will it take her to save up $600? Explain your method for finding the answer.

30) **Extended Response** Jillian has to read 125 pages to finish a book for class. It needs to be finished in 8 days. Amelia said, "If you read 14 pages a night for the next 8 nights, you will finish the book." Is Amelia correct? Explain your answer using words or numbers.

Exponents

Key Ideas

Exponents provide a short way to indicate the number of times a number is used as a factor.

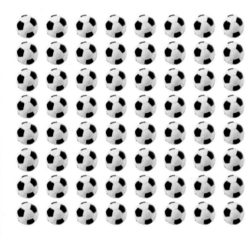

How many bowling balls do you see?

$8 + 8 + 8 = 24$
$3 \times 8 = 24$

How many soccer balls are there?

$8 + 8 + 8 + 8 + 8 + 8 + 8 + 8 = 64$
$8 \times 8 = 64$

We can write this another way.
$8^2 = 64$

Here, the 2 is called an exponent. The 8 is called the base of the exponent.

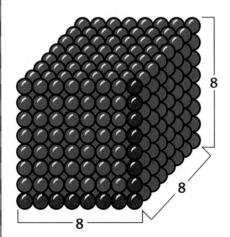

How many racquet balls are there?
A layer has 8 racquet balls in each row and column. So, there are 64 racquet balls in each layer. In total, there are 8 layers (of 64 racquet balls each).

$8 \times 64 = 8 \times 8 \times 8 = 512$
$8^3 = 512$

Here, 8 is still the base, but the exponent is 3. What does the 3 mean?

The 3 means to use 8 as a factor 3 times.

eTextbook This lesson is available in the *eTextbook*.

Solve these exercises.

1 **a.** $1^7 = $ ▢   **b.** $7^1 = $ ▢

2 **a.** $2^3 = $ ▢   **b.** $3^2 = $ ▢

3 **a.** $3^4 = $ ▢   **b.** $4^3 = $ ▢

4 **a.** $3^5 = $ ▢   **b.** $5^3 = $ ▢

5 **a.** $2^4 = $ ▢   **b.** $4^2 = $ ▢

6 **a.** $1^{10} = $ ▢   **b.** $10^1 = $ ▢

7 **a.** $2^6 = $ ▢   **b.** $6^2 = $ ▢

Answer these questions.

8 Do you think it is true that when you add any two numbers you can add them in any order? For instance, does $4 + 2$ equal $2 + 4$? Does this work for all numbers you can think of?

9 Do you think it is true that when you multiply any two numbers you can multiply them in any order? For instance, does 3×6 equal 6×3? Does this work for all numbers you can think of?

10 **Extended Response** Do you think it is true that for any two numbers n and m, $n^m = m^n$? For instance, does 2^3 equal 3^2? Describe what you learned from Exercises 1–7 about this.

Use exponents to complete these number sentences.
For example $4 \times 4 \times 4 \times 4 \times 4 = 4^5$

11 $2 \times 2 \times 2 \times 2 \times 2 \times 2 = $ ▢   **12** $7 \times 7 = $ ▢

13 $4 \times 4 \times 4 \times 4 \times 4 \times 4 \times 4 = $ ▢   **14** $5 \times 5 \times 5 \times 5 = $ ▢

15 $8 \times 8 \times 8 \times 8 \times 8 = $ ▢   **16** $9 \times 9 \times 9 \times 9 \times 9^3 = $ ▢

17 $10 \times 10 \times 10 \times 10 = $ ▢   **18** $1{,}000 \times 10 = $ ▢

Writing + Math   **Journal**
Can you find a case where $n^m = m^n$?

Workout

If you have ever run up and down the court for more than a few minutes, you know that the game of basketball can be quite a workout.

But exactly what kind of workout is it? To find out, a team of researchers in Australia placed electronic monitors on eight basketball players. Then they measured the heart rate and movements of the players as they ran, jumped, and shuffled their way through a series of games. The researchers used different categories to describe what the players were doing at any given moment.

It turns out that the players spent the most time in less vigorous activities like standing and walking.

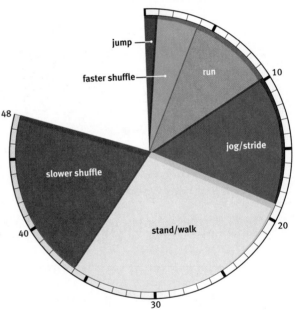

The researchers used *different categories* to describe what the players were doing at any given moment.

52

The researchers also made a graph to show how often a player's heart beat at different rates. The graph shows the results for the 48 minutes that the clock was running during each game.

Researchers' conclusion: Even though the players spent less time in more vigorous activities like running and jumping, their heart rate was high most of the time.

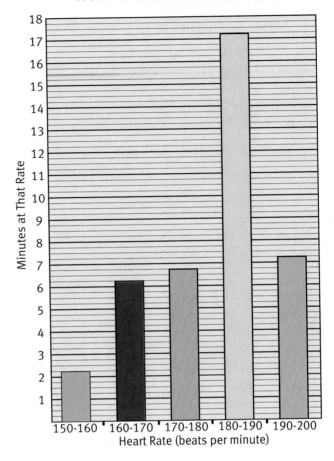

How Fast Their Hearts Beat

Minutes at That Rate

Heart Rate (beats per minute)

53

Solve these problems. Use the graphs on both pages to help you.

1 For about how many minutes did a player's heart beat between 180 and 190 beats per minute?

2 About what fraction of the time was the heart rate 180 beats per minute or faster?

3 On the graph of heart rates, do the times add up to 48 minutes? How can you explain that?

4 Is the graph on page 230 a useful way to display the data? How else could you show the same data?

5 Do you agree with the researchers' conclusion? Why do you think this result happened?

Exploring 💡 Problem Solving

How fast does your heart beat when you exercise? How long does it take to return to its resting rate? Follow these steps to find out.

A. Measure and record the heart rate of each person in your group. To save time, use the method shown.

B. Have one person choose an activity from below and do it for 1 minute.

C. Measure and record the person's heart rate every minute for 10 minutes.

D. Repeat steps B and C for each person in your group.

E. Make a line graph to show how your heart rate changed during the 10 minutes after your exercise.

Measure how many times you feel a pulse in 15 seconds.

Multiply to find the rate for 1 minute.

Running in place   Jumping in place   Shuffling feet fast   Jumping jacks

Answer these questions.

6. Did everyone in your group have the same heart rate before exercising?

7. Did everyone in your group have the same heart rate after exercising?

8. How were the graphs in your group alike? How were they different?

9. How long did it take to return to your resting heart rate?

10. How does this experiment help you explain the researcher's conclusion on page 231?

ⓔ Textbook This lesson is available in the *eTextbook*.

Multiply. Use shortcuts when you can.

1) $\begin{array}{r} 43 \\ \times\ 54 \\ \hline \end{array}$ ▪

2) $\begin{array}{r} 96 \\ \times\ 27 \\ \hline \end{array}$ ▪

3) $\begin{array}{r} 58 \\ \times\ 5 \\ \hline \end{array}$ ▪

4) $\begin{array}{r} 18 \\ \times\ 67 \\ \hline \end{array}$ ▪

5) $\begin{array}{r} 420 \\ \times\ 20 \\ \hline \end{array}$ ▪

6) $\begin{array}{r} 21 \\ \times\ 20 \\ \hline \end{array}$ ▪

7) $\begin{array}{r} 86 \\ \times\ 59 \\ \hline \end{array}$ ▪

8) $\begin{array}{r} 39 \\ \times\ 9 \\ \hline \end{array}$ ▪

9) $\begin{array}{r} 58 \\ \times\ 50 \\ \hline \end{array}$ ▪

10) $\begin{array}{r} 47 \\ \times\ 35 \\ \hline \end{array}$ ▪

11) $\begin{array}{r} 39 \\ \times\ 90 \\ \hline \end{array}$ ▪

12) $\begin{array}{r} 13 \\ \times\ 29 \\ \hline \end{array}$ ▪

Solve these problems.

13) Students from Kennedy School are going on a field trip. There are 525 people going. Each bus can seat 45 people. It costs $85 to rent each bus for 1 day.

  a. Will 12 buses be too few, just enough, or too many?

  b. How many extra seats will there be?

  c. How much will it cost to rent 12 buses for 1 day?

14) Kwame bought 16 stamps at 37¢ each. How much did Kwame pay? Give your answer in cents, then in dollars and cents.

15) A hotel room costs $46 for 1 night. How much would it cost to stay at the hotel for 11 nights?

16) Olivia's dad bought cheeseburgers for the entire soccer team. One cheeseburger costs 89¢. Olivia's dad bought 24 of them. He gave the cashier $25. How much change should he get back?

Applying Multiplication

Key Ideas

Multiplication can be used to solve many problems in real-life situations.

For example:

Tony wants to buy 3 CDs. He has $25.

Each CD costs $9. Does Tony have enough for the 3 CDs?

To find out, Tony multiplies 9 by 3.

$9 \times 3 = 27$

Therefore, Tony does not have enough money for 3 CDs.

Solve these problems.

1 A rectangle is 63 meters long and 42 meters wide.

    a. What is the area of the rectangle?

    b. What is the perimeter of the rectangle?

2 Yusef bought 6 quarts of milk. Each quart cost 77¢.

    a. How many cents did he pay for the 6 quarts?

    b. How much did he pay in dollars and cents?

ⓔTextbook This lesson is available in the *eTextbook*.

3 Tara bought 5 muffins. Each muffin cost 72¢. How much did she pay for the 5 muffins? Give your answer in cents and then in dollars and cents.

4 Matt owns 6 dogs. Each dog weighs about 32 kilograms. Do they weigh more than 240 kilograms altogether?

5 Each of Matt's dogs can jump over a stream that is about 350 centimeters wide without getting wet. About how wide a stream can they jump together?

6 A rectangle is 32 centimeters long and 63 centimeters wide.

    a. What is the area of the rectangle?

    b. What is the perimeter of the rectangle?

7 There are 24 bottles of orange juice in 1 case. How many bottles are in 6 cases?

8 There are 100 centimeters in 1 meter. How many centimeters are in 7 meters?

9 A school has 15 buses. Each bus seats 66 students.

    a. How many students can be seated on the buses at once?

    b. If the school has a population of 752, how many seats are empty on each day that all the students use the bus?

A bottle of soda costs 65¢ at Terwilliger's Drugstore. At the One-Stop Food Shop, you can buy a case of 24 bottles of soda for $16.56. If you return a bottle to the recycling center, you get back 5¢.

Answer these questions.

10 Bryan wants to buy 48 bottles of soda. How much will he have to pay at Terwilliger's Drugstore?

11 How much will 48 bottles cost at the One-Stop Food Shop?

12 How much would Bryan save by buying his soda at the One-Stop Food Shop instead of Terwilliger's?

13 How much money will Bryan get back when he recycles the 48 bottles?

14 **Extended Response** Kelvin and Niki have found 21 empty soda bottles. When they return them to the recycling center, will they get enough money to buy 3 bottles of soda at Terwilliger's? Explain your answer.

e Textbook This lesson is available in the *eTextbook*.

  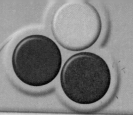 

Game

Multidigit Multiplication and Strategies Practice

Four Cube Multiplication Game

Players: Two or more

Materials: *Number Cubes:* two 0–5 (red), two 5–10 (blue)

Object: To get the greatest product

Math Focus: Multidigit multiplication, place value, and mathematical reasoning

HOW TO PLAY

1 Take turns rolling all four **Number Cubes.** If a 10 is rolled, roll that cube again.

2 Combine the numbers you rolled to make a two-digit by two-digit or a three-digit by one-digit multiplication problem

For example, if you rolled: 8 5 7 3

These are some problems you could make:

853	73	753	75
× 7	× 85	× 8	× 83

3 The player with the greatest product wins. (Find the exact products only if you need to.)

SAMPLE GAME

Terri rolled: 4 2 7 8

She made this problem:

82
× 74

Jun rolled: 3 0 6 5

He made this problem:

53
× 60

Terri won the round. (Terri and Jun did not have to find the exact products to see that Terri's product was greater.)

 **Journal**

If the digits 7, 5, 3, and 2 were rolled, and you followed the same rules as the **Four Cube Multiplication Game,** what would be the least product that you could create? How did you find your answer?

Multiplication Practice

Key Ideas

Sometimes you need to find an exact product of two two-digit numbers. If you cannot think of a shortcut, remember the steps you can use that will always work.

$$\begin{array}{r} 36 \\ \times\ 45 \\ \hline 180 \end{array}$$

First, multiply the top number (36) by the digit in the **ones** column of the bottom number (5).

$36 \times 5 = 180$

....

$$\begin{array}{r} 36 \\ \times\ 45 \\ \hline 180 \\ 144 \end{array}$$

Next, multiply the top number (36) by the digit in the **tens** column of the bottom number (4).

$36 \times 4 = 144$

....

$$\begin{array}{r} 36 \\ \times\ 45 \\ \hline 180 \\ 144 \\ \hline 1620 \end{array}$$

Finally, add to get the final answer.

Multiply. Use shortcuts when you can.

1
$$\begin{array}{r} 90 \\ \times\ 90 \\ \hline \end{array}$$
■

2
$$\begin{array}{r} 68 \\ \times\ 49 \\ \hline \end{array}$$
■

3
$$\begin{array}{r} 96 \\ \times\ 17 \\ \hline \end{array}$$
■

4
$$\begin{array}{r} 32 \\ \times\ 90 \\ \hline \end{array}$$
■

5
$$\begin{array}{r} 55 \\ \times\ 25 \\ \hline \end{array}$$
■

6
$$\begin{array}{r} 38 \\ \times\ 43 \\ \hline \end{array}$$
■

7
$$\begin{array}{r} 72 \\ \times\ 95 \\ \hline \end{array}$$
■

8
$$\begin{array}{r} 87 \\ \times\ 70 \\ \hline \end{array}$$
■

9
$$\begin{array}{r} 71 \\ \times\ 70 \\ \hline \end{array}$$
■

10
$$\begin{array}{r} 63 \\ \times\ 91 \\ \hline \end{array}$$
■

11
$$\begin{array}{r} 18 \\ \times\ 22 \\ \hline \end{array}$$
■

12
$$\begin{array}{r} 30 \\ \times\ 31 \\ \hline \end{array}$$
■

13
$$\begin{array}{r} 66 \\ \times\ 36 \\ \hline \end{array}$$
■

14
$$\begin{array}{r} 76 \\ \times\ 41 \\ \hline \end{array}$$
■

15
$$\begin{array}{r} 57 \\ \times\ 43 \\ \hline \end{array}$$
■

e Textbook This lesson is available in the *eTextbook*.

Solve these problems.

16 The ice-cube maker in Zack's refrigerator makes 14 ice cubes every hour. How many ice cubes can it produce in 12 hours?

17 Yuki's soccer team is selling magazine subscriptions to raise money. They can keep 35¢ for each subscription they sell. If the 14 members sell 1 subscription each, how much money will they raise?

18 Kala's father wants to put a rectangular trampoline in the backyard. The trampoline is 12 feet wide and 11 feet long, and the backyard is 15 feet wide and 16 feet long. How much square footage will be left in the backyard after the trampoline is installed?

Note: There are many ways to recognize that the answer to a problem is wrong. Sometimes the size of the answer is so far off that it is clearly impossible. Sometimes the last digit of an answer is impossible.

Decide which of the given answers is correct by showing that the other two could not be correct.

19 $42 \times 16 = $ ▨
a. 640
b. 672
c. 58

20 $395 \times 87 = $ ▨
a. 34,365
b. 334,305
c. 43,427

21 $145 \times 15 = $ ▨
a. 2,320
b. 2,160
c. 2,175

22 $79 \times 2,583 = $ ▨
a. 21,344
b. 312,054
c. 204,057

23 $3,598 + 8,745 = $ ▨
a. 21,344
b. 18,433
c. 12,343

24 $872,558 - 4,444 = $ ▨
a. 888,113
b. 868,114
c. 8,214

25 $7,682 + 297 = $ ▨
a. 7,979
b. 7,385
c. 7,987

26 $482,100 - 165,000 = $ ▨
a. 647,100
b. 342,000
c. 317,100

27 $8,742 - 2,952 = $ ▨
a. 5,790
b. 5,802
c. 5,831

28 $852 + 258 = $ ▨
a. 1,111
b. 111
c. 1,110

29 $64 \times 38 = $ ▨
a. 2,470
b. 2,432
c. 2,560

30 $35 \times 4 = $ ▨
a. 160
b. 140
c. 120

Writing + Math **Journal**

A student in your class is having difficulty multiplying two two-digit numbers together. Help this student by explaining how to multiply two two-digit numbers together.

Key Ideas

Multiplying a three-digit number by a two-digit number is very similar to multiplying a two-digit number by a two-digit number.

Marla's aunt Rosa is getting married. Marla has been helping by using her math skills. Rosa invited 376 people to the wedding. Rosa is expecting to pay $23 for dinner for each person invited. How much money is Marla's aunt going to pay for all the dinners?

Multiply: 23×376

$$\begin{array}{r} 376 \\ \times\ 23 \\ \hline 1128 \end{array}$$

Start at the right. Multiply the top number by the **ones** digit.

$3 \times 376 = 1,128$

There are 1,128 **ones.**

Write 1,128 so that the digit on the right (8) is in the **ones** column.

· ·

$$\begin{array}{r} 376 \\ \times\ 23 \\ \hline 1128 \\ 752 \end{array}$$

Multiply by the **tens** digit.

$2 \times 376 = 752$

There are 752 **tens.**

Write 752 so that the digit on the right (2) is in the **tens** column.

· ·

$$\begin{array}{r} 376 \\ \times\ 23 \\ \hline 1128 \\ 752 \\ \hline 8648 \end{array}$$

Add to get the final answer.

Marla's aunt is going to spend $8,648 for dinner at her wedding.

Check to see that the answer makes sense.

This lesson is available in the *eTextbook*.

The answer should be less than 30 × 400, which is 12,000.

The answer should be greater than 20 × 300, which is 6,000.

8,648 is less than 12,000 and greater than 6,000. So the answer makes sense.

Multiply: 30 × 312

Here's how you would multiply using the method shown on page 256. We're going to follow a similar path by starting on the right, because it's easier.

312 × 30 ‾‾‾‾ 0	Multiply the top number by the **ones** digit. 0 × 312 = 0 Write 0 in the **ones** column.

- -

312 × 30 ‾‾‾‾ 0 936	Multiply by the **tens** digit. 3 × 312 = 936 There are 936 **tens.** Write 936 so the digit on the right (6) is placed in the **tens** column.

- -

312 × 30 ‾‾‾‾ 0 936 ‾‾‾‾ 9360	Add.

Here's a shorter way to multiply 30 × 312.

312 × 30 ‾‾‾‾ 0	Multiply the top number by the **ones** digit. 0 × 312 = 0 Write 0 in the **ones** column.

- -

312 × 30 ‾‾‾‾ 9360	Multiply by the **tens** digit. 3 × 312 = 936 There are 936 **tens.** Write the 936 next to the 0.

Remember:

387 × 46	→	387 × 46 ‾‾‾‾ 2322	→	387 × 46 ‾‾‾‾ 2322 1548	→	387 × 46 ‾‾‾‾ 2322 1548 ‾‾‾‾ 17802

Multiply. Use shortcuts when you can.

① 247
× 26

② 813
× 59

③ 512
× 64

④ 256
× 32

⑤ 243
× 27

⑥ 806
× 37

⑦ 281
× 7

⑧ 281
× 70

⑨ 394
× 8

⑩ 394
× 80

⑪ 38
× 27

⑫ 380
× 27

⑬ 7
× 8

⑭ 70
× 8

⑮ 700
× 8

Solve these problems.

⑯ How many days are in 14 years (there are 365 days in 1 year), 3 of which are leap years (366 days)?

⑰ Derek averaged 16 points for his basketball team in every game they played.

a. How many points will he have scored if he played in 12 games?

b. **Extended Response** At this rate, about how many games would it take for him to score 1,000 points? Explain how you found your answer.

⑱ A local movie theater sold 345 tickets for a movie. If each person spends $14 on a ticket, popcorn, and a soda, how much money will the theater make?

⑲ There are 42 rows of bleachers in the school gym. At the pep rally there were 30 people sitting in each row. How many people were sitting at the pep rally?

⑳ Andrew's family drove 264 miles to the beach for summer vacation. They returned home using the same route. How many miles did they travel?

Textbook This lesson is available in the *eTextbook*.

Give the dimensions of a rectangle that fits these numbers. If there is no such rectangle, explain why. Use a calculator if needed.

Example: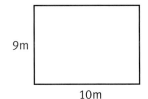

9m

10m

perimeter = 38m, area = 90 sq. m

Answer: length = 10m, width = 9m

Check: 10 + 9 + 10 + 9 = 38, and 10 × 9 = 90

㉑ perimeter = 20 cm, area = 24 sq. cm

㉒ perimeter = 202 m, area = 100 sq. m

㉓ perimeter = 26 m, area = 36 sq. m

㉔ perimeter = 24 cm, area = 36 sq. cm

㉕ perimeter = 36 m, area = 81 sq. m

㉖ perimeter = 30 cm, area = 56 sq. cm

㉗ perimeter = 4 m, area = 1 sq. m

㉘ perimeter = 16 m, area = 16 sq. m

㉙ perimeter = 40 cm, area = 36 sq. cm

㉚ perimeter = 74 m, area = 36 sq. m

Solve these problems.

Tim's vegetable garden is 14 meters long and 11 meters wide.

㉛ What is the perimeter of Tim's garden?

㉜ What is the area of Tim's garden?

A rectangle has a length of 496 cm and a width of 24 cm.

㉝ What is the perimeter of the rectangle?

㉞ What is the area of the rectangle?

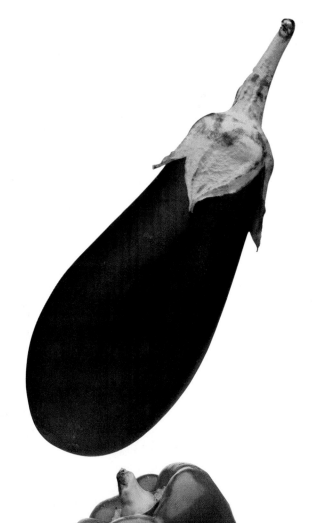

Mr. Jones is planning to make a display in his pet store by stacking cans of dog food in the shape of a pyramid. He wants to make the pyramid as tall as possible. He has 10 cases of dog food with 24 cans in each case.

- How many layers high can he make the pyramid?

- How many cans will he use in the bottom layer?

Aisha solved the problem this way:

I started to solve the problem by Making a Model and using Guess, Check, and Adjust.

1. Get 240 cubes.

2. Build a stack like the one in the picture, only bigger.

3. See if I use all the cubes.

4. If I have more cubes, I'll try building a bigger stack.

Think about Aisha's strategy. Answer these questions.

1 Why did Aisha decide to get 240 cubes?

2 According to the picture, how many layers will be in Aisha's stack?

3 If this stack does not have enough cubes, will Aisha be able to keep the stack and just add another layer?

4 Would you use Aisha's strategy to solve the problem? Explain.

    e Textbook This lesson is available in the *eTextbook*.

Sean solved the problem this way:

I also Made a Model to help solve the problem. But then I Made a Table and Looked for a Pattern.

1. Get some cubes.

2. Build a few layers.

3. Look for a pattern in the number of cans in each layer.

4. Use the pattern to find how many layers can be made with 240 cans.

Think about Sean's strategy. Answer these questions.

5. In the stack Mr. Jones is making, how many cans will be in the third layer from the top?

6. How many cans will be in the fourth layer from the top?

7. What pattern do you see in the number of cans in each layer?

8. Will the pattern continue? Why?

9. Do you think Sean's strategy will work? Why or why not?

10. Use Aisha's strategy, Sean's strategy, or a strategy of your own to solve the problem. What strategy did you use? Why?

Cumulative Review

Adding and Subtracting Integers **Lesson 2.9**

Solve.

1. In the morning the temperature was −4 degrees. It warmed up 15 degrees to reach the high temperature of the day. What was the high temperature?

2. When Shamus went to bed the temperature outside was 16 degrees. When he woke the next morning he noticed the thermometer read −6. By how much did the temperature change?

. . . .

Multiplying by Powers of 10 **Lesson 5.1**

Replace *n* with the correct answer.

3. $100 \times 5 = n$

4. $1,000 \times 8 = n$

5. $1,000 \times 2 = n$

6. $1,000 \times 37 = n$

7. $100 \times 49 = n$

8. $10 \times 781 = n$

. . . .

Multiplication and Division **Lesson 3.10**

Solve.

9. $20 \div 2 =$ ▢
   a. 40
   b. 10
   c. 5

10. $36 \div 6 =$ ▢
    a. 9
    b. 8
    c. 6

11. $7 \times 8 =$ ▢
    a. 54
    b. 56
    c. 58

12. $24 \div 8 =$ ▢
    a. 4
    b. 6
    c. 3

13. $56 \div 8 =$ ▢
    a. 7
    b. 5
    c. 6

14. $4 \times 12 =$ ▢
    a. 24
    b. 36
    c. 48

15. $6 \times 7 =$ ▢
    a. 48
    b. 42
    c. 36

16. $35 \div 7 =$ ▢
    a. 4
    b. 5
    c. 6

e Textbook This lesson is available in the *eTextbook*.

Solve each problem.

20 Each week Julie's parents give her $12 for an allowance. How many weeks will it take for her to save $149 for a video game system?

21 There are 16 ounces in 1 pound. The new Colossal-Mega Burger weighs 3 pounds. How many ounces does it weigh?

22 Darion is a running back for his football team. His season is 12 games long. In the first game he carried the ball 18 times for 57 yards.

    a. If he ran the ball 18 times each game, how many carries would he have altogether?

    b. If he ran for 57 yards each game, how many yards would he have for the season?

23 Theresa received $75 for her birthday. At Shop-A-Lot she bought a CD player for $20. Now she wants to figure out how many CDs she can buy for $12 each.

24 **Extended Response** Explain how you would approximate 123×456.

Lesson 6.10

Juice spilled on these exercises. Choose the correct answer in each case.

25
$$\begin{array}{r} 45 \\ \times\ 6 \\ \hline \end{array}$$
    a.   2400
    b. 28,086
    c. 260,345

26
$$\begin{array}{r} 8\,6 \\ -\ 3 \\ \hline \end{array}$$
    a. 531
    b. 1106
    c. 1276

27
$$\begin{array}{r} 146 \\ \times\ 4 \\ \hline \end{array}$$
    a. 6278
    b. 4504
    c. 1464

Multiply.

1. 83
   × 42

Ⓐ 6,348   Ⓑ 3,486

Ⓒ 125   Ⓓ 4,836

2. 348
   × 57

Ⓐ 19,836   Ⓑ 1,983

Ⓒ 13,896   Ⓓ 16,832

3. 417
   × 192

Ⓐ 800,064   Ⓑ 8,064

Ⓒ 80,064   Ⓓ 80,004

4. 72
   × 33

Ⓐ 105   Ⓑ 216

Ⓒ 2,376   Ⓓ 3,376

5. 85
   × 64

Ⓐ 149   Ⓑ 510

Ⓒ 5,349   Ⓓ 5,440

6. 622
   × 58

Ⓐ 4,976   Ⓑ 36,076

Ⓒ 36,766   Ⓓ 46,076

7. 243
   × 61

Ⓐ 14,823   Ⓑ 14,581

Ⓒ 12,248   Ⓓ 1,701

8. 2,574
   × 246

Ⓐ 30,088   Ⓑ 423,508

Ⓒ 624,294   Ⓓ 633,204

Add or subtract.

9. 624
   + 382

Ⓐ 906   Ⓑ 960

Ⓒ 1,006   Ⓓ 1,016

10. 712
   − 443

Ⓐ 269   Ⓑ 271

Ⓒ 296   Ⓓ 331

ⓔ **Textbook**   This lesson is available in the *eTextbook*.

Choose the correct answer.

11. What is the perimeter of a classroom that is 25 feet long and 16 feet wide?

    (A) 9 feet   (B) 82 feet

    (C) 86 feet   (D) 400 feet

12. What is the area of a cafeteria that measures 58 feet long and 37 feet wide?

    (A) 95 square feet

    (B) 190 square feet

    (C) 2,146 square feet

    (D) 2,461 square feet

13. How many inches are in 6 feet?

    (A) 72 inches   (B) 84 inches

    (C) 90 inches   (D) 108 inches

14. How many cups are in 4 gallons?

    (A) 16 cups   (B) 32 cups

    (C) 44 cups   (D) 64 cups

Some digits are covered. One answer is correct. Select the letter of the correct answer.

15.   403
      − 2▨

    (A) 98   (B) 149

    (C) 222   (D) 255

16.   411
      × 7▨

    (A) 2,877   (B) 149

    (C) 32,058   (D) 255

17.   112
      × 6▨

    (A) 64,308   (B) 74,810

    (C) 67,622   (D) 75,600

Which symbol makes the sentences true?

18. 320 ▨ 413 − 88

    (A) =

    (B) >

    (C) <

19. 320 + 35 ▨ 189 + 163

    (A) =

    (B) >

    (C) <

Practice Test

Solve for n.

20. $48 \div (9 - 3) = n$

Ⓐ $n = 2$ Ⓑ $n = 4$

Ⓒ $n = 6$ Ⓓ $n = 8$

21. $5 + (3 \times 4) = n$

Ⓐ $n = 17$ Ⓑ $n = 20$

Ⓒ $n = 60$ Ⓓ $n = 72$

Choose the best answer.

22. $3 \times 3 \times 3 \times 3 = $ ▢

Ⓐ 3^4 Ⓑ 4^3

Ⓒ 27 Ⓓ 12

23. $5^3 = $ ▢

Ⓐ 15 Ⓑ 25

Ⓒ 125 Ⓓ 225

Solve the problems.

24. Mark needs 3 yards of material for his kite. He has 3 feet of blue material and 2 feet of red material. His mother gave him 15 inches of yellow material. A friend had 9 inches of green material left from his last project. How much more material does Matt need?

Ⓐ 2 feet Ⓑ 10 feet

Ⓒ 1 foot Ⓓ 6 feet

25. There are 28 mints in a bag. How many mints are in 15 bags?

Ⓐ 420 Ⓑ 640

Ⓒ 42 Ⓓ 240

26. Chris bought 24 balloons. If each balloon costs 59¢, how much did Chris spend on balloons?

Ⓐ $16.14 Ⓑ $14.16

Ⓒ $11.14 Ⓓ $11.16

27. The hotel ordered 19 boxes of new guest towels, with 24 towels in each box. How many towels did the hotel order?

Ⓐ 465 Ⓑ 566

Ⓒ 654 Ⓓ 456

28. Juan has 3 pounds of walnuts. How many ounces of walnuts does he have?

Ⓐ 4 ounces Ⓑ 84 ounces

Ⓒ 48 ounces Ⓓ 8 ounces

29. Kirsta is making punch for her friends. She needs to add 3 quarts of water to the mix. She has added 6 cups of water. How much more water should she add?

Ⓐ 2 cups Ⓑ 4 cups

Ⓒ 8 cups Ⓓ 6 cups

Ⓔ **Textbook** This lesson is available in the *eTextbook*.

Extended Response ▶ **Solve** the problems below. Explain how you found each answer.

30. The playground at school is 140 feet long and 75 feet wide.

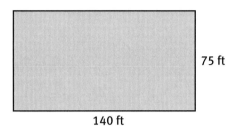

75 ft

140 ft

a. What is the perimeter of the playground?

b. What is the area of the playground?

c. Draw a sketch of a playground that has a greater perimeter, but a smaller area than the one at your school. Find the perimeter and area of the playground you sketched. Be sure to show your work.

Introduction to Fractions, Decimals, and Percentages

In This Chapter You Will Learn

- about the relationship between percents and fractions.
- how to calculate percents.
- how to use stopwatches to explore decimals, percents, and fractions.

Problem Solving

The Arctic is a region that is rich in beauty and natural resources. It includes parts of the United States and many other countries. The graphs on the map show how many people from different countries live in the Arctic. The graphs also show that many of these inhabitants, especially from the United States and Canada, have immigrated to the Arctic.

SOCIAL STUDIES

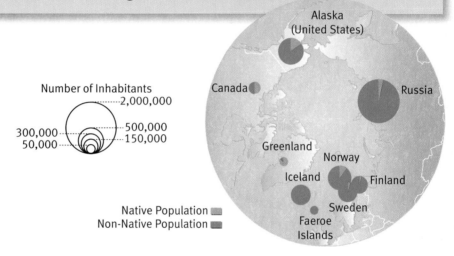

Number of Inhabitants
2,000,000
500,000
300,000
150,000
50,000

Native Population ▮
Non-Native Population ▮

Work in groups to answer these questions.

1. Which country has more people living in the Arctic, the United States or Canada?

2. Which country has more native inhabitants in the Arctic, the United States or Canada?

3. Suppose you randomly chose two people living in the Arctic, one from the United States and one from Canada. Which of the two people would more likely be native to the Arctic? Explain.

Key Ideas

Percent means "out of 100."

How could you find 75% full with your string?

100% of 1 = 1   50% of 1 = $\frac{1}{2}$ of 1   25% of 1 = $\frac{1}{4}$ of 1   75% of 1 = $\frac{3}{4}$ of 1

A beaker can be filled with liquid to different levels. The height of the liquid relates to how full the beaker is. This percent full can be thought of in standard percentages that are easy to recognize: 100% full (completely full), 50% full (half full), 25% full (one-quarter full) and 75% full (three-quarters full).

Imagine a string stretched to the full height of a beaker. If we folded this string in half, it would stretch to the 50% full level. If we folded it in half again, or quartered it, it would stretch to the 25% full level. One way to find 75% full with your string is to imagine shortening the string by 25%. Try to think of other ways.

Percentages are used in many situations in our daily lives. Several examples are shown here.

e Textbook This lesson is available in the *eTextbook*.

For each excercise write *true* if the percentage written below the beaker correctly shows how full it is. If you think a label is *false,* explain what you believe the correct percentage to be.

1. 50% full
2. 25% full
3. 75% full
4. 60% full

5. 5% full
6. 35% full
7. 10% full
8. 30% full

 **Journal**

Explain in your own words the meaning of the word *percent.*

Key Ideas

Half of something and 50% of something are the same. Similarly, one quarter of something and 25% of something are the same.

Some percentages, such as 100%, 50%, 25%, and 75%, are easier to work with than others. Percentages like these make good reference points. We call them benchmarks. The beakers below illustrate these benchmark percentages.

Because we know the actual height of the liquid in the first beaker, we can use our knowledge about percentages and their equivalent fractions to find the actual heights of the liquid in the other beakers.

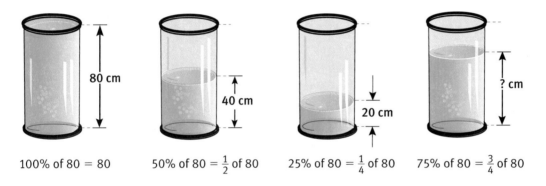

100% of 80 = 80   50% of 80 = $\frac{1}{2}$ of 80   25% of 80 = $\frac{1}{4}$ of 80   75% of 80 = $\frac{3}{4}$ of 80

Suppose an 80-centimeter tall beaker was half full. That would mean the height of the liquid was 50% of 80, or half of 80, which is 40 centimeters.

If it was 25% full, the height would be half of the 50% height, or half of 40 centimeters, which is 20 centimeters.

Draw four rectangles (12 cm × 2 cm) on a separate sheet of paper. These four rectangles will be your set of beakers. Label the beakers with the following percentages: 100%, 50%, 25%, and 75%. Estimate the location of the percent line on each beaker, and use a pencil to mark the spot. Use your ruler to measure the height of the beaker in centimeters, and then use this measurement to find the exact percent line. Show that line with a marker.

Complete.

1 100% of 12 = ▢   **2** 50% of 12 = ▢

3 25% of 12 = ▢   **4** 75% of 12 = ▢

Solve the following exercises.

5 50% of 80 = ▢   **6** 25% of 80 = ▢   **7** 75% of 80 = ▢

8 $\frac{1}{2}$ of 200 = ▢   **9** $\frac{1}{4}$ of 200 = ▢   **10** $\frac{3}{4}$ of 200 = ▢

11 50% of 16 = ▢   **12** 25% of 16 = ▢   **13** 75% of 16 = ▢

14 $\frac{1}{2}$ of 44 = ▢   **15** $\frac{1}{4}$ of 44 = ▢   **16** $\frac{3}{4}$ of 44 = ▢

Solve the following exercises.

17 25% of 12 = ▢   **18** $\frac{1}{4}$ of 16 = ▢   **19** 75% of 8 = ▢

20 $\frac{1}{2}$ of 24 = ▢   **21** $\frac{3}{4}$ of 20 = ▢   **22** $\frac{1}{4}$ of 60 = ▢

23 $\frac{1}{2}$ of 54 = ▢   **24** 75% of 120 = ▢

25 Clownfish are orange with black and white stripes and live near coral reefs in the wild. Jehan wanted a clownfish that was $24. Jehan had saved a total of $18 when the pet store announced a sale. The sale was 25% off the regular price of all fish in the store. Do you think that Jehan can afford the clownfish at the sale price? Will it cost her all of her savings, or will she get change?

Understanding $12\frac{1}{2}$% and $\frac{1}{8}$

Key Ideas

One-eighth of something and $12\frac{1}{2}$% of something are the same.

100% of 120 = 120

50% of 120 = $\frac{1}{2}$ of 120

25% of 120 = $\frac{1}{4}$ of 120

$12\frac{1}{2}$% of 120 = $\frac{1}{8}$ of 120

Finding $12\frac{1}{2}$%

Example: Let's find $12\frac{1}{2}$% of 120.

Step 1: Find 100% of the number. 100% of 120 = 120

Step 2: Half of 100% is 50%. Find half of the number.
50% of 120 (half of 120) = 60

Step 3: Half of 50% is 25%. Find half of your previous answer. 25% of 120 (half of 60) = 30

Step 4: Half of 25% is $12\frac{1}{2}$%. Find half of your previous answer. $12\frac{1}{2}$% of 120 (half of 30) = 15

Find $12\frac{1}{2}$% of the following quantities.

1 $12\frac{1}{2}$% of 16 = ▢

2 $12\frac{1}{2}$% of 80 = ▢

3 $12\frac{1}{2}$% of 40 = ▢

4 $12\frac{1}{2}$% of 24 = ▢

5 $12\frac{1}{2}$% of 32 = ▢

6 $12\frac{1}{2}$% of 200 = ▢

Create your own problem.

7 $12\frac{1}{2}$% of ▢ = ▢

Give an equivalent fraction for each percentage or an equivalent percentage for each fraction.

8 50% of 1 = ◻

9 $\frac{3}{4}$ of 1 = ◻

10 $12\frac{1}{2}$% of 1 = ◻

11 $\frac{1}{4}$ of 1 = ◻

Compare the statements below, and answer true or false. If the answer is false, explain what would make the statement true. The first one is done for you.

12 50% of 4 $< \frac{3}{4}$ of 4   true

13 $12\frac{1}{2}$% of 24 $< \frac{1}{4}$ of 24

14 75% of 1 $> \frac{3}{4}$ of 1

15 $\frac{1}{8}$ of 8 $<$ 25% of 8

16 $\frac{3}{4}$ of 20 $<$ 80% of 20

17 10% of 100 $> \frac{1}{8}$ of 100

Look at the following exercises. Answer if the statement is true or false. If it is false, write the correct percentage or fraction for the right side of the equation.

18 25% of 1 + 25% of 1 $= \frac{1}{2}$ of 1

19 $12\frac{1}{2}$% of 1 + 25% of 1 $= \frac{1}{4}$ of 1

20 $\frac{3}{4}$ of 1 + $\frac{1}{8}$ of 1 = 100% of 1

21 $\frac{1}{4}$ of 1 + $\frac{1}{2}$ of 1 = 75% of 1

22 25% of 1 + 75% of 1 = 1

23 100% of 1 − 25% of 1 $= \frac{1}{2}$ of 1

Cumulative Review

Multiplication and Division Lessons 3.1–3.11

Multiply or divide.

1 9 ÷ 3

2 6 × 4

3 24 ÷ 8

4 7 × 5

5 12 ÷ 12

6 12 ÷ 1

7 7 × 7

8 36 ÷ 6

9 6 × 7

10 14 ÷ 3

11 10 × 8

12 2 × 9

13 3 × 11

14 24 ÷ 5

15 49 ÷ 6

Common Multiples and Common Factors Lesson 3.12

List all the factors of each number, and find the greatest common factor.

16 15 and 18

17 36 and 32

18 20 and 16

List the first three common multiples for each pair of numbers.

19 3 and 4

20 6 and 5

21 7 and 2

Cumulative Review

Lessons 5.3, 6.1, and 6.4

Solve the following problems.

22 Jacob's car is 7 feet wide and 12 feet long. How many square feet will be left if he parks in a parking space that is 9 feet wide and 18 feet long?

23 Stephanie is putting a lattice fence around the bottom portion of her deck. Her deck is shaped like an octagon, and each side is 6 feet long. How many feet of lattice will she need to surround her deck?

24 Melinda placed $1.50 in her piggy bank and was curious to see how much she could save in a month. At the end of the month, to her surprise, she had 10 times more than what she started with. How much money did Melinda have?

25 While at the mall, Miguel found a square stand for his new phone. The phone is 12 centimeters by 9 centimeters and the stand is 11 centimeters on all sides. Should Miguel buy this stand? Explain why or why not.

26 $78 \times 100 = $ ▢

27 $35 \times 10 = $ ▢

28 $100 \times 3 = $ ▢

29 $325 \times 200 = $ ▢

30 $43 \times 500 = $ ▢

Adding and Subtracting Integers Lesson 2.9

Decide whether the answer is correct or not. If it is wrong, correct it.

31 $-6 + -3 = -9$

32 $6 + (-5) = 1$

33 $12 + (-7) = -5$

34 $-14 + -6 = 20$

35 $9 + (-9) = 0$

36 $18 + (-5) = -13$

Key Ideas Review

In this chapter you determined how decimals and percentages are similar.

You learned how to find a percentage of a whole number.

You learned how decimals can be placed on a number line and how to determine if one decimal is greater than another.

Solve the following problems.

1. 25% of $40 = $ ☐

2. 100% of $25 = $ ☐

3. 10% of $60 = $ ☐

4. 75% of $36 = $ ☐

Place the following decimals in order from least to greatest.

5. 0.74, 1.04, 1.65, 0.76, and 1.26

6. 12.65, 12.56, 1.26, 0.12, and 125.6

7. 0.62, 0.6, 0.58, 0.55, and 0.7

How large is the difference between the two decimals?

8. 0.78 and 0.25

9. 12.36 and 1.98

Solve the exercise below.

10. **Extended Response** How would you find 25% of 40?

Lessons 7.1 and 7.2

Answer the following in percents.

1 This beaker is:

   a. 25% full

   b. 100% full

   c. 75% full

   d. 50% full

3 This beaker is:

   a. 25% full

   b. 10 % full

   c. 100% full

   d. 75% full

2 This beaker is:

   a. 100% full

   b. 25% full

   c. 50% full

   d. 75% full

4 This beaker is:

   a. 50% full

   b. 25% full

   c. 100% full

   d. 75% full

Lessons 7.2, 7.3, and 7.8

Solve for n.

5 50% of 30 = n

6 $\frac{1}{8}$ of 320 = n

7 0.25 of 400 = n

8 $12\frac{1}{2}$ % of 24 = n

9 0.75 of 160 = n

10 10% of 160 = n

11 $\frac{1}{10}$ of 270 = n

12 20% of 150 = n

13 0.50 of 1,000 = n

14 25% of 24 = n

15 $\frac{1}{2}$ of 420 = n

16 75% of 80 = n

Lesson 7.6

Find the difference.

17 0.35 − 0.28 =

18 0.46 − 0.12 =

19 3.66 − 1.77 =

20 0.49 − 0.03 =

21 2.11 − 1.09 =

22 7.02 − 3.49 =

e Textbook This lesson is available in the *eTextbook*.

Solve each problem.

23 Julio bought a skateboard for $25. He got the skateboard at 50% off the original price. What was the original price?

24 One eighth of Mrs. Smith's class was absent on Monday. If she has 24 students in her class, how many were absent?

25 Tonya ran a race against Patrick. Tonya's time was 6.54 seconds, while Patrick's time was 7.02 seconds. How much time passed between Tonya's and Patrick's finishes?

26 **Extended Response** Raven went to the store to buy a purse. She had $20. The purse she liked was originally $28 but is now 25% off.

a. Does she have enough money for the purse?

b. How do you know?

Lesson 7.6

27 James's shooting statistics for the last four basketball games were: 33%, 0.42, $\frac{18}{36}$, and $\frac{5}{20}$. Arrange his statistics in order from least to greatest.

28 **Extended Response** Micah bought a pair of shoes at 50% off. A week later at another store, he saw the same shoes for only 25% off, but the shoes cost less than his. How is this possible?

Use the number line to answer questions 1 through 4.

0   1

1. Where does the bar start?

2. Where does the bar end?

3. What is the length of the bar?

4. What percentage of the total length is the bar's length?

Solve the problems below. Be sure to show your work.

Four pencils that are each 7 centimeters long can be placed end to end. Their overall length equals the length of a book.

5. What percentage of the length of the book is each stick?

6. What is the length of the book?

Janet wants to buy a video game for $50. She found a coupon in the newspaper for 30% off the current price.

7. How much money will Janet save if she uses the coupon?

8. How much will the video game cost Janet with the coupon?

e Textbook This lesson is available in the *eTextbook*.

Select the correct answer.

9. How full is the beaker?

   Ⓐ 15%   Ⓑ 25%

   Ⓒ 55%   Ⓓ 90%

10. What is 10% of 30?

    Ⓐ 3   Ⓑ 10

    Ⓒ 15   Ⓓ 30

11. What is 75% of 64?

    Ⓐ 8   Ⓑ 16

    Ⓒ 48   Ⓓ 60

12. What is $\frac{3}{4}$ of 12?

    Ⓐ 2   Ⓑ 6

    Ⓒ 9   Ⓓ 10

13. What is $12\frac{1}{2}$% of 200?

    Ⓐ 10   Ⓑ 12

    Ⓒ 20   Ⓓ 25

Which symbol makes the statement true?

14. 20% of 17 ▮ 40% of 9

    Ⓐ =   Ⓑ >

    Ⓒ <

15. 75% of 12 ▮ $\frac{1}{2}$ of 48

    Ⓐ =   Ⓑ >

    Ⓒ <

16. LaDawn ran 10 meters in 47 centiseconds. Mary ran 10 meters in 50 centiseconds. How much faster was LaDawn ?

    Ⓐ 0.33 seconds   Ⓑ 0.30 second

    Ⓒ 0.03 seconds   Ⓓ 0.003 seconds

17. What is the difference between 3.89 and 3.01?

    Ⓐ 0.60   Ⓑ 0.64

    Ⓒ 0.88   Ⓓ 0.91

18. What is 10% of 90?

    Ⓐ 0.9   Ⓑ 9

    Ⓒ 90   Ⓓ 900

19. What is 10% of 500?

Ⓐ 0.05　　Ⓑ 0.5

Ⓒ 5　　　　Ⓓ 50

20. Which could be a rule for this function?

64 —(?)→ 16

Ⓐ −30　　Ⓑ ÷ 4

Ⓒ ÷ 8　　Ⓓ × 4

21. Which could be a rule for this function?

50 —(?)→ 60

Ⓐ − 10　　Ⓑ + 10

Ⓒ ÷ 2　　　Ⓓ × 3

22. How many ounces are in 80 pounds?

Ⓐ 160　　Ⓑ 320

Ⓒ 640　　Ⓓ 1,280

23. How many inches are in 3 yards?

Ⓐ 36　　Ⓑ 78

Ⓒ 108　　Ⓓ 216

24. How many pints are in 4 gallons?

Ⓐ 16　　Ⓑ 24

Ⓒ 32　　Ⓓ 44

Multiply.

25.
$$812 \times 715$$

Ⓐ 463,170　Ⓑ 475,195

Ⓒ 550,280　Ⓓ 580,580

26.
$$3,210 \times 473$$

Ⓐ 515,280　Ⓑ 518,330

Ⓒ 1,518,330　Ⓓ 1,528,330

Divide.

27.
$$5\overline{)72}$$

Ⓐ 14　　　Ⓑ 14R2

Ⓒ 15　　　Ⓓ 15R3

28.
$$8\overline{)57}$$

Ⓐ 7　　　Ⓑ 7R1

Ⓒ 7R3　　Ⓓ 8R1

ⓔ **Textbook** This lesson is available in the *eTextbook.*

Extended Response **Solve** the problems below.

29. A full beaker is shown below.

    a. Draw pictures to show beakers that are 25%, 50%, and 75% full. Label each beaker.

    b. If the height of the liquid in the full beaker is 60 centimeters, what is the height of the liquid in the other three beakers? Explain how you found each answer.

30. Blake made coffee mugs and sold them at the flea market. He spent $12 on the supplies, and sold the mugs for a total of $90. Because Jillian helped Blake for a little while, Blake told Jillian that she could have either 11% of the total sales, or $13\frac{1}{4}$% of the profits. Which payment method should Jillian choose? Explain your answer.

CHAPTER 8 Fractions, Probability, and Measurement

6512

U.S. COAST GUARD

In This Chapter You Will Learn
- how to investigate probability by using fractions.
- about equivalent fractions and mixed numbers.
- how to add and subtract fractions.

Problem Solving

Old methods and modern technology can work together to save lives. Imagine you and a friend are on a hiking trip. Your friend is lost and uses a walkie-talkie to contact you.

I don't know where I am, but this may help. If I face the sun and then turn clockwise three-quarters of a complete turn, I'm facing the top of the mountain. If I face the sun and then turn clockwise one-third of a complete turn, then I'm facing the top of the tow . . .

Suddenly the signal gives out. There is silence. You take out your map and look toward the sun, which is directly north.

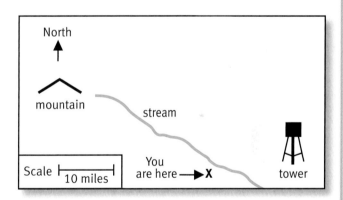

Copy the map. Then answer these questions.

1. What fraction of a complete counterclockwise turn would be the same as turning clockwise $\frac{3}{4}$ of a complete turn?

2. What compass direction is your friend facing when he or she faces the mountaintop?

3. Is your friend north or south of the stream? Explain.

4. Draw a horizontal line on your map to show how far north or south your friend is. Use the rest of the information to determine your friend's location.

Key Ideas

Fractions can be used to describe a part of a whole.

The bottom number of a fraction, the denominator, tells how many equal-sized parts there are in the whole or set. The top number of a fraction, the numerator, describes how many of those equal-sized parts to consider.

numerator $\longrightarrow$ $\dfrac{2}{5}$
denominator $\longrightarrow$

What fraction of each of the following figures has been shaded?

1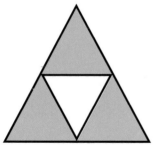

2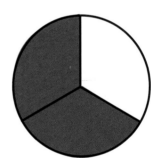

3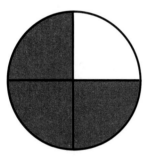

4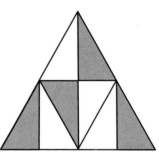

5

6

e Textbook This lesson is available in the *eTextbook*.

Using Relation Signs **Lesson 2.4**

What is the correct sign? Write $<$, $>$, or $=$.

10 $100 \ \boxed{} \ 73 + 10$

11 $24 - 6 \ \boxed{} \ 16 + 8$

· ·

Percent Benchmarks **Lesson 7.2**

Solve.

12 $50\% \text{ of } 44 = \boxed{}$

13 $75\% \text{ of } 180 = \boxed{}$

· ·

Understanding 10% and $\frac{1}{10}$ **Lesson 7.8**

Complete the following problems.

14 $30\% \text{ of } 90 = \boxed{}$

15 $60\% \text{ of } 90 = \boxed{}$

· ·

Rounding **Lesson 1.4, 1.8**

Solve the following problems.

16 A rectangle has a length of 10 inches and a width of 6 inches. Find the perimeter of this rectangle. Draw two new rectangles that have the same perimeter but different measurements.

17 The city baseball team had an attendance of 6,858 at the first game of the season and 5,923 at the second game. Round each game's attendance to the nearest hundred, and estimate the total number of fans in attendance for both games.

Fractions Greater than 1

Key Ideas

There are different ways to write fractions greater than 1 or rational numbers greater than 1.

One way is to write a whole number plus a fraction less than 1. This is sometimes called a mixed number. For example, $2\frac{1}{8}$ is a mixed number that means 2 whole quantities plus $\frac{1}{8}$.

Another way is to write a fraction with a top number (numerator) greater than its bottom number (denominator). This is sometimes called an improper fraction. An example of an improper fraction is $\frac{17}{8}$.

Here is an example of how to use a mixed number.

Mr. Cheng baked 4 loaves of bread.

His children ate half of one loaf. Mr. Cheng had three and one-half loaves left.

We can write three and one half as $3\frac{1}{2}$.

Write a mixed number to show how many.

1

◻ apples

2

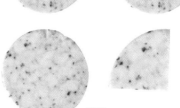

◻ cheese wheels

ⓔ Textbook This lesson is available in the **eTextbook**.

Mr. Cheng cut the remaining loaves of bread into half-loaves and told his children they were allowed to eat one half-loaf per day. Mr. Cheng now has 7 half-loaves left.

We can write seven halves as $\frac{7}{2}$.

If Mr. Cheng's children do as he asked, how long will the bread last?

Write an improper fraction to show how many.

3

[ ] apples

4

[ ] cheese wheels

Since mixed numbers and improper fractions can both be used to represent the same amount, you can use whichever form is most convenient.

Look at the following example of how to write $2\frac{3}{5}$ as an improper fraction:

- The denominator of the new improper fraction will be the same as the denominator of the fraction in the mixed number. In this example, the denominator is 5 (fifths).

- Determine how many fifths there are in the whole number part (the 2) of the mixed number. Count the number of parts in the picture below or multiply 2 by 5. The answer is 10. $\frac{10}{5}$ is equivalent to 2 whole units.

Can you see that $2\frac{3}{5}$ and $\frac{13}{5}$ represent the same amount in the picture below?

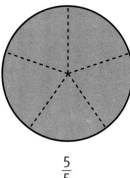   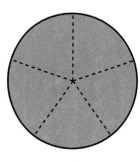   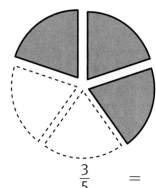

$$\frac{5}{5} \quad + \quad \frac{5}{5} \quad + \quad \frac{3}{5} \quad = \quad \frac{13}{5}$$

$\frac{10}{5}$ (the whole-number part) $+ \frac{3}{5}$ (the fraction part) $= \frac{13}{5}$

Write each mixed number as an improper fraction.

5. $2\frac{5}{6}$

6. $4\frac{1}{3}$

7. $3\frac{1}{6}$

8. $4\frac{3}{5}$

9. $6\frac{5}{9}$

10. $2\frac{5}{7}$

11. $3\frac{1}{4}$

12. $3\frac{5}{6}$

13. $5\frac{3}{8}$

14. $2\frac{3}{8}$

15. $4\frac{3}{4}$

16. $1\frac{2}{5}$

Look at the following example of how to write the improper fraction $\frac{13}{5}$ as a mixed number:

- How many whole units are there in $\frac{13}{5}$, or how many groups of 5 are in 13? The answer is 2 whole units.

- Notice the leftover amount is $\frac{3}{5}$.

- The improper fraction $\frac{13}{5}$ can be rewritten as 2 whole units and $\frac{3}{5}$, or $2\frac{3}{5}$.

Can you see that $\frac{13}{5}$ and $2\frac{3}{5}$ represent the same number in the picture below?

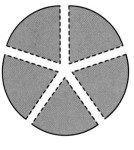   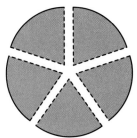   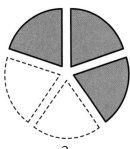

$$1 \quad + \quad 1 \quad + \quad \frac{3}{5} \quad = \quad 2\frac{3}{5}$$

Write each improper fraction as a mixed number or a whole number.

17 $\frac{5}{2}$ 18 $\frac{5}{4}$ 19 $\frac{8}{6}$ 20 $\frac{7}{5}$

21 $\frac{21}{3}$ 22 $\frac{15}{7}$ 23 $\frac{29}{3}$ 24 $\frac{8}{7}$

25 $\frac{7}{4}$ 26 $\frac{11}{6}$ 27 $\frac{20}{5}$ 28 $\frac{28}{5}$

Writing + Math **Journal**

Find the improper fraction that is equal to the mixed number $4\frac{5}{6}$. Draw a picture that shows what it means.

Key Ideas

There are many ways to name rational numbers greater than 1.

- Fractions greater than 1

- Decimal equivalents greater than 1

- Percents greater than 100%

To find a fraction that is equivalent to another, multiply the starting fraction by another fraction that is equal to 1. Remember, a fraction is equal to 1 when the numerator and denominator are the same.

$$\frac{3}{4} \times \frac{2}{2} = \frac{6}{8}$$

The process is the same for an improper fraction.

$$\frac{11}{5} \times \frac{2}{2} = \frac{22}{10}$$

The fractions $\frac{11}{5}$ and $\frac{22}{10}$ are equivalent fractions and represent the same amount. The fractions are different ways to express the same rational number.

Fill in the missing information to make the following statements true.

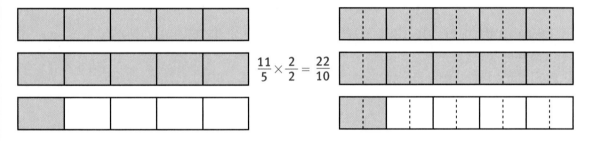

1. $\frac{7}{3} = \frac{\blacksquare}{12}$

2. $\frac{5}{2} = \frac{20}{\blacksquare}$

3. $\frac{9}{4} = \frac{\blacksquare}{20}$

4. $\frac{13}{6} = \frac{\blacksquare}{18}$

5. $\frac{8}{5} = \frac{24}{\blacksquare}$

6. $\frac{\blacksquare}{8} = \frac{44}{32}$

To find an **equivalent** fraction for a mixed number, you would first write it as an improper fraction. You may then multiply the improper fraction by a fraction that is equal to 1. Look at the following example:

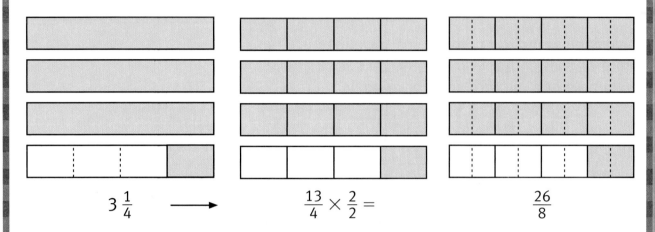

$$3 \frac{1}{4} \longrightarrow \qquad \frac{13}{4} \times \frac{2}{2} = \qquad \frac{26}{8}$$

The mixed number $3\frac{1}{4}$ can be written as the equivalent improper fraction $\frac{13}{4}$. It may then be multiplied by a fraction equal to 1 (in this example, $\frac{2}{2}$ was used). So another equivalent fraction for $3\frac{1}{4}$ is $\frac{26}{8}$, which also can be written as $3\frac{2}{8}$.

Fill in the missing information to make the following statements true.

7. $\frac{9}{8} = \frac{\blacksquare}{64}$

8. $\frac{7}{1} = \frac{\blacksquare}{7}$

9. $\frac{\blacksquare}{2} = \frac{48}{32}$

10. $\frac{18}{\blacksquare} = \frac{36}{14}$

11. $1\frac{9}{10} = \frac{\blacksquare}{100}$

12. $2\frac{2}{5} = \frac{36}{\blacksquare}$

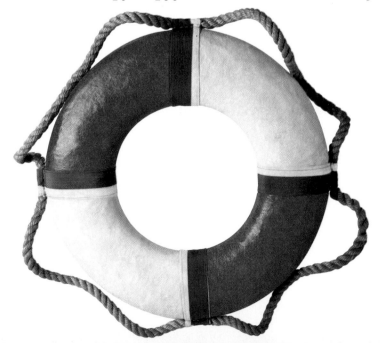

We have already learned that we can use fractions less than 1 to name locations on the number line between 0 and 1. In exactly the same way as we did for fractions less than 1, we are able to name locations on the number line using fractions greater than 1.

We can extend our number line by using either mixed numbers or improper fractions. Let's look at the following example of a number line from 1 to 3:

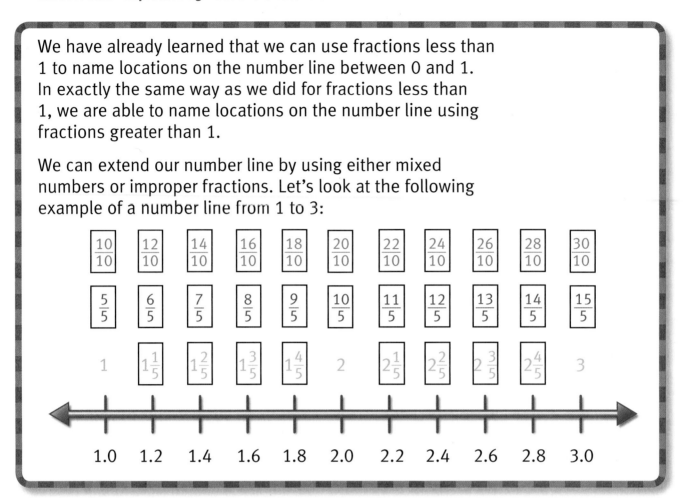

Use what you have learned about finding equivalent fractions and about decimal equivalents to solve the following exercises. Use the number line to help you.

What is the decimal equivalent of

13. $\frac{6}{5}$ 14. $\frac{26}{10}$ 15. $2\frac{3}{5}$ 16. $\frac{14}{10}$ 17. $1\frac{2}{5}$

18. $\frac{30}{15}$ 19. $\frac{36}{20}$ 20. $\frac{18}{15}$ 21. $2\frac{2}{10}$ 22. $\frac{36}{10}$

Remember that rational numbers can be graphed on the number line. Therefore, $\frac{24}{10}$, $\frac{12}{5}$, $2\frac{2}{5}$, and 2.4 are all names for the same rational number, and they are graphed at the same point on the number line.

Select the correct answer.

7. What is $\frac{1}{2}$ of $\frac{6}{8}$?

   Ⓐ $\frac{1}{8}$ 　 Ⓑ $\frac{3}{8}$

   Ⓒ $\frac{4}{10}$ 　 Ⓓ $\frac{2}{10}$

8. Dakota can save $\frac{1}{4}$ of the cost of a tennis racket when it goes on sale. How much will she save on a racket that regularly costs $70?

   Ⓐ $7.00 　 Ⓑ $12.50

   Ⓒ $17.00 　 Ⓓ $17.50

9. Which fraction is equivalent to $\frac{4}{9}$?

   Ⓐ $\frac{4}{16}$ 　 Ⓑ $\frac{12}{32}$

   Ⓒ $\frac{8}{18}$ 　 Ⓓ $\frac{2}{3}$

10. Which decimal is equivalent to $\frac{4}{5}$?

    Ⓐ 0.3 　 Ⓑ 0.5

    Ⓒ 0.6 　 Ⓓ 0.8

11. Which answer shows $\frac{19}{5}$ written as a mixed number?

    Ⓐ $1\frac{9}{5}$ 　 Ⓑ $2\frac{2}{3}$

    Ⓒ $3\frac{4}{5}$ 　 Ⓓ $5\frac{4}{6}$

12. About how long is the crayon?

    Ⓐ $2\frac{1}{4}$ inches 　 Ⓑ $2\frac{1}{2}$ inches

    Ⓒ $3\frac{4}{5}$ inches 　 Ⓓ $5\frac{4}{6}$ inches

13. Jennie has 12 cousins, and 2/3 of them are girls. How many of her cousins are girls?

    Ⓐ 2 　 Ⓑ 3

    Ⓒ 8 　 Ⓓ 5

14. Craig ran 2 miles on Wednesday and $3\frac{1}{4}$ miles on Saturday. How many miles did he run altogether?

    Ⓐ $1\frac{1}{4}$ 　 Ⓑ $5\frac{1}{4}$

    Ⓒ $5\frac{1}{2}$ 　 Ⓓ 5

Solve for *n*.

15. $\frac{2}{3} \times \frac{1}{8} = n$

    Ⓐ $n = \frac{1}{12}$ Ⓑ $n = \frac{6}{12}$

    Ⓒ $n = \frac{6}{7}$ Ⓓ $n = \frac{8}{9}$

16. $\frac{4}{7} \times \frac{1}{2} = n$

    Ⓐ $n = \frac{1}{2}$ Ⓑ $n = \frac{3}{7}$

    Ⓒ $n = \frac{2}{7}$ Ⓓ $n = \frac{3}{10}$

17. What is 20% of 80?

    Ⓐ 8   Ⓑ 10

    Ⓒ 16   Ⓓ 24

18. What is 5% of 80?

    Ⓐ 12   Ⓑ 4

    Ⓒ 3   Ⓓ 2

Use the graph to answer questions 19 through 21.

19. What are the coordinates of point *D*?

    Ⓐ (2, 9)   Ⓑ (3, 2)

    Ⓒ (9, 2)   Ⓓ (9, 5)

20. What point is at (3, 5)?

    Ⓐ A   Ⓑ B

    Ⓒ D   Ⓓ C

21. What is the length of segment *AE*?

    Ⓐ 5   Ⓑ 6

    Ⓒ 9   Ⓓ 12

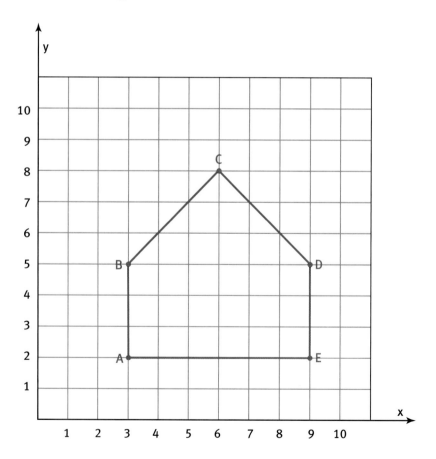

ⓔ **Textbook** This lesson is available in the *eTextbook*.

Extended Response **Solve** the problems below.

22. In a game, each player rolls two cubes numbered 0 to 5. The player adds the value of each cube and records the score. After 10 rolls, the player with the most points wins.

a. Complete the table to show all the possible sums of the two cubes.

b. How many possible outcomes are there?

c. What is the highest sum a player can roll?

d. What is the probability that a player will roll the sum of 5?

e. What is the probability that a player will get no points on a given turn?

	0	1	2	3	4	5
0						
1						
2						
3						
4						
5						

CHAPTER 9

Decimals and Measurement

In This Chapter You Will Learn

- about strategies for comparing decimals.
- about the relationships among metric units.
- how to add, subtract, and multiply decimals.

Problem Solving

John took a survey to see which television shows students in his grade watched. He picked three of his favorite shows. He asked all 100 fourth graders in his school whether they watched these shows last week. He also asked if they watched any show during those times. He recorded his results in a table.

TV Show	Day	Time	Number Who Watched This Show	Number Who Watched TV at this Time
My Friend Max	Sat.	9:00 – 9:30 a.m.	19	54
Halftime	Tues.	7:30 – 8:00 p.m.	21	83
Space Kids	Sun.	1:00 – 1:30 p.m.	5	10

Work with a group to answer these questions.

1. What fraction of all fourth graders watched each show?

2. About what fraction of fourth graders who were watching television watched each show?

3. Which show do you think is most popular? Why?

4. If a company wants to put a commercial on television, it pays the station or the network. The price depends on the show. Why do you think it costs so much more to put on a commercial during *Halftime* than during *Space Kids?*

Prices for a 30-Second Commercial	
TV Show	Price
My Friend Max	$50,000
Halftime	$100,000
Space Kids	$5,000

5. If you were putting a commercial on television, which show would you choose in order to get the most value for your money? Explain.

Key Ideas

You can write numbers between 0 and 1 in different ways.

"I just made up a game," said June. "What's the least number greater than 0 that you can make?"

"I know," shouted Andy. "It's 1."

"I can do better than that," said Rico. "I say $\frac{1}{2}$."

"That's not fair," said Andy. "We can't use that kind of number."

"It's my game," said June. "Any kind of number is all right. And I'm going to say $\frac{1}{10}$."

"Well," said Andy, "I can make a number that's even less."

Which of the following might Andy use as an example?

 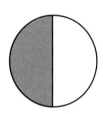 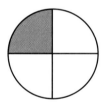

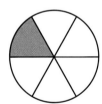  

The last three figures ($\frac{1}{12}$, $\frac{1}{16}$, and $\frac{1}{20}$) are examples of numbers less than $\frac{1}{10}$.

Textbook This lesson is available in the *eTextbook*.

If you divide a whole into ten equal parts, each part is one-tenth of the whole.

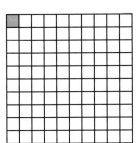

We can write one-tenth in different ways:

As a fraction: $\frac{1}{10}$

As a decimal: 0.1

$\frac{1}{10} = 0.1$

When you read 0.1, you say "one tenth" or "zero point one."

If you divide a whole number into one hundred equal parts, each part is one-hundredth of the whole.

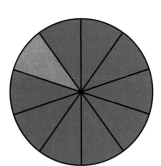

We can write one-hundredth in two ways:

As a fraction: $\frac{1}{100}$

As a decimal: 0.01

$\frac{1}{100} = 0.01$

When you read 0.01, you say "one one-hundredth" or "zero point zero one."

Answer these questions.

1. Suppose you divide 1 into 1,000 equal parts. What would each part be? Write it in two ways.

2. Suppose you divide 1 into 10,000 equal parts. Show two ways to write what each part would be.

3. Suppose you divide 1 into 100,000 equal parts. Show two ways to write what each part would be.

4. Suppose you divide 1 into 1,000,000 equal parts. Show two ways to write what each part would be.

5. Which is greater, $\frac{1}{10}$ or $\frac{1}{100}$?

6. Which is greater, 0.1 or 0.01?

7. Which is greater, 0.1 or 0.001?

Our system of writing numbers is based on 10. Look at the number 3,333.

The red 3 stands for 3 ones.

- What does the orange 3 stand for? 3 tens

- What does the green 3 stand for? 3 hundreds

- What does the blue 3 stand for? 3 thousands

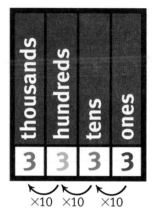

As we move to the left, each place is worth 10 times as much.

A 3 in the tens place is worth 10 times the value of a 3 in the ones place.

A 3 in the hundreds place is worth 10 times a 3 in the tens place.

If you move to the right, it's just the opposite. Each place is worth one-tenth as much.

A 3 in the tens place is worth one-tenth of a 3 in the hundreds place.

A 3 in the ones place is worth one-tenth of a 3 in the tens place.

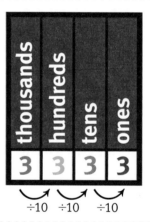

- What happens if you keep going to the right?

The next place is worth one-tenth of 1. That's the tenths place.

- What happens if you keep going to the right?

The next place is worth one-tenth of one-tenth. That's the hundredths place.

- How do you know what place you are in? The decimal point tells where the ones place is and you can determine the value of the placeholder by counting the digits to the right or left of the ones place.

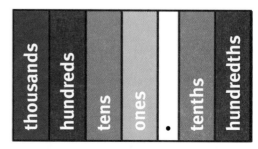

e Textbook This lesson is available in the *eTextbook*.

Use a point between the ones place and the tenths place.

The point is called a decimal point.

Suppose you want to write 4 tens, 3 ones, 5 tenths, and 4 hundredths.

You would write it like this: 43.54

When written in this form the number is called a decimal.

When you read it, you would say "forty-three and fifty-four hundredths" or "forty-three point fifty four."

Tell the value of the bold digit in each of the following numbers.

8 0.0**5**

9 1.**6**3

10 **2**0.37

11 62.**7**6

12 74.3**5**

13 0.**5**7

14 **2**.59

15 91.3**5**

16 **5**3.47

17 22.2**2**

18 **1**.6

19 83.5**6**

20 21.4**2**

21 17.**5**2

22 15.**0**6

Write each number in standard decimal form.

23 5 ones, 2 tenths, 4 hundredths

24 7 hundreds, 2 tens, 6 ones, 3 tenths

25 3 tens, 3 ones, 3 tenths, 3 hundredths

26 9 hundreds, 0 tens, 3 ones, 4 tenths, 5 hundredths

27 4 tens, 9 ones, 0 tenths, 7 hundredths

Write each number in standard decimal form. The first one has been done for you.

28 30 + 4 + 0.6 + 0.04 34.64

29 16 + 0.8 + 0.05

30 60 + 0 + 0.7 + 0.03

31 80 + 2 + 0.06

32 50 + 9 + 0.3 + 0.07

33 90 + 1 + 0.7 + 0.02

34 10 + 3 + 0.9 + 0.06

35 20 + 4 + 0.8 + 0.06

Decimals and Fractions

Key Ideas

Decimals make numbers easy to compare.

Remember, if a whole is divided into 10 equal parts, 1 part would be $\frac{1}{10}$, or 0.1.

So, 3 parts would be $\frac{3}{10}$, or 0.3.

$\frac{1}{10} = 0.1$

$\frac{3}{10} = 0.3$

If a whole is divided into 100 equal parts, 1 part would be $\frac{1}{100}$, or 0.01.

So, 3 parts would be $\frac{3}{100}$, or 0.03.

$\frac{1}{100} = 0.01$

$\frac{3}{100} = 0.03$

Suppose you divided a whole into 1,000 equal parts.

- What would 1 part be?
  $\frac{1}{1,000}$ or 0.001
- What would 3 parts be?
  $\frac{3}{1,000}$ or 0.003
- What would 7 parts be?
  $\frac{7}{1,000}$ or 0.007

Here is one way to compare the decimals 0.007 and 0.03.

0.007

0.03**0**

So 0.007 < 0.03 (as $\frac{7}{1,000} < \frac{30}{100}$).

Write a 0 after the last digit so the numbers have the same number of digits to the right of the decimal point.

Line up the decimal points.

Replace ▮ with <, >, or =.

1 0.1 ▮ 0.3

2 0.03 ▮ 0.1

3 0.007 ▮ 0.08

4 0.01 ▮ 0.03

5 0.7 ▮ 0.08

6 0.2 ▮ 0.09

7 0.01 ▮ 0.07

8 0.1 ▮ 0.001

9 0.3 ▮ 0.03

e Textbook This lesson is available in the *eTextbook*.

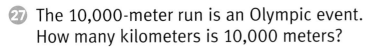

26 In the 1900 Olympics, J. W. B. Tewksbury ran the 400-meter hurdle in 57.6 seconds. In 1992 Kevin Young had a time of 46.78 seconds in the same event. How much faster was Young?

27 The 10,000-meter run is an Olympic event. How many kilometers is 10,000 meters?

28 In the 2004 Olympics, Kaitlin Sandeno swam the 400-meter freestyle in 4 minutes and 6.19 seconds. In the 1924 Olympics, John Weissmuller swam the 400-meter freestyle in 5 minutes and 4.2 seconds. By how much did Kaitlin Sandeno beat John Weissmuller's time?

29 In the 1964 Olympics, Abebe Bikila ran the marathon *barefoot* in 2 hours, 12 minutes, and 11.2 seconds. (The marathon is 42,195 m—about 26 miles!) In the 1948 Olympics, Delfo Cabrera ran the marathon in 2 hours, 34 minutes, and 51.6 seconds. In how much less time did Abebe Bikila run the marathon barefoot?

30 In the 1932 Olympics, Volmari Iso-Hollo ran an extra lap by mistake in the 3,000-meter steeplechase. His time for the race was 10 minutes and 33.4 seconds. In the 1936 Olympics, he ran the same race in 9 minutes and 3.8 seconds. About how long do you think it took Iso-Hollo to run the extra lap?

 **Journal**

When adding whole numbers such as 123 + 45, are the decimals aligned? Explain your answer.

IN THE 1940S

Old TV shape

New TV shape

In the 1940s, when television first came out, companies decided to make television screens the same shape as movie screens.

Years later, movie screens became wider. Eventually, the shape of television screens changed, too.

Imagine that you are designing a portable movie player. You want to use the widescreen format. You want the screen to be 5.00 centimeters high. How wide should it be?

Ken solved the problem this way:

I Used Simpler Numbers and Made a Table to solve the problem.

How would I solve the problem if the numbers were simpler? What if the ratio were 2 to 1 instead of 1.78 to 1?

I could make a table to show the widths for different heights.

Height	1 cm	2 cm	3 cm
Width	2 cm	4 cm	6 cm

I can use the same kind of table with the actual ratio 1.78 to 1.

Height	1.00 cm	2.00 cm	3.00 cm
Width	1.78 cm	3.56 cm	

ⓔ **Textbook** This lesson is available in the **eTextbook.**

Think about Ken's strategy. Answer these questions.

1. Why does Ken's first table show a width of 2 centimeters for a height of 1 centimeter?

2. Why does the second table show a width of 1.78 centimeters for a height of 1 centimeter?

3. In the second table, what is the meaning of 3.56 centimeters? How do you think Ken got that figure?

Beverly solved the problem this way:

I Made a Diagram and Used a Pattern to solve the problem.

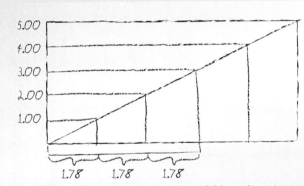

Every time the screen gets 1 cm higher, it gets 1.78 cm wider.

Think about Beverly's strategy. Answer these questions.

4. What does Beverly's diagram show?

5. Why did Beverly draw all the rectangles with the same shape?

6. What pattern do you see for the width of the screens?

7. How can Beverly finish solving the problem?

8. How is Beverly's strategy like Ken's strategy? How is it different?

9. Solve the problem. What strategy did you use? Why?

Cumulative Review

Multidigit Addition and Subtraction Lesson 2.3

Solve each problem.

①
$$\begin{array}{r} 364165 \\ +\ 381632 \\ \hline \end{array}$$

②
$$\begin{array}{r} 10000 \\ -\ \ \ 854 \\ \hline \end{array}$$

....

Fractions and Rational Numbers Lesson 8.3

Write two equivalent fractions for the following.

③ $\dfrac{4}{10}$

④ $\dfrac{3}{15}$

⑤ $\dfrac{6}{7}$

....

Composite Function Rules Lesson 4.10

⑥ $36 \div 3 = \blacksquare$

⑦ $8 \times 6 = \blacksquare$

⑧ $0 \div 144 = \blacksquare$

⑨ $8 \times 7 = \blacksquare$

⑩ $10 \times 20 = \blacksquare$

....

Two- and Three-Digit Multiplication Lessons 6.2 and 6.5

⑪
$$\begin{array}{r} 58 \\ \times\ 16 \\ \hline \end{array}$$

⑫
$$\begin{array}{r} 411 \\ \times\ 64 \\ \hline \end{array}$$

⑬
$$\begin{array}{r} 800 \\ \times\ 15 \\ \hline \end{array}$$

⑭
$$\begin{array}{r} 616 \\ \times\ 812 \\ \hline \end{array}$$

⑮
$$\begin{array}{r} 393 \\ \times\ 127 \\ \hline \end{array}$$

....

Adding and Subtracting Fractions Greater than 1 Lesson 8.15—8.16

Solve the following exercises. Write answers greater than 1 as mixed numbers or whole numbers.

⑯ $3\dfrac{1}{3} + 7\dfrac{1}{3} = n$

⑰ $4\dfrac{13}{16} - 3\dfrac{3}{4} = n$

⑱ $\dfrac{1}{5} + 2\dfrac{3}{10} = n$

⑲ $n = 4\dfrac{2}{3} - 3\dfrac{1}{7}$

⑳ $\dfrac{5}{4} + 3\dfrac{1}{4} = n$

㉑ $6\dfrac{5}{9} - \dfrac{13}{9} = n$

㉒ $8 + 2\dfrac{3}{7} = n$

ⓔ Textbook This lesson is available in the *eTextbook*.

Applying Fractions Lesson 8.6

Solve.

(23) $\frac{2}{6}$ of 24 = ▢

(24) $\frac{1}{5}$ of 35 = ▢

(25) $\frac{6}{12}$ of 50 = ▢

(26) $\frac{1}{7}$ of 28 = ▢

(27) $\frac{1}{9}$ of 54 = ▢

Using Relations Signs Lesson 2.4

What is the correct sign, <, >, or =?

(28) $54 \div 9 + 3$ ▢ 1×10

(29) $15 \times 15 - 30$ ▢ 35

(30) $6 \times 8 + 12$ ▢ 12×5

(31) $92 - 20 \div 8$ ▢ 3

(32) $64 \div 4 - 12$ ▢ 5

Percent Benchmarks Lesson 7.2

Solve.

(33) 75% of 80 = ▢

(34) 25% of 25 = ▢

(35) 30% of 50 = ▢

(36) 15% of $120 = ▢

(37) Vivian bought 1 new CD at the mall today. The price tag on the CD read $15.00 (including tax). However, when she gave the sales clerk $15.00, the clerk said, "Oh, these are on sale today." She gave Vivian $2.25 in change. Figure out what the percentage off the price was.

Comparing Fractions Lesson 8.9

Place the fractions on the number line.

0   1

(38) $\frac{1}{2}$

(39) $\frac{3}{4}$

(40) $\frac{1}{6}$

(41) $\frac{2}{3}$

(42) $\frac{12}{12}$

Key Ideas

Many different situations involve decimal numbers.

Use your skills for working with decimals to solve the following problems.

1 A year ago Jake bought a used car that had traveled 48,927.8 miles. Now the car has traveled 75,485.2 miles.

  a. How many miles has the car traveled in the past year?

  b. How many miles does the car need to travel to reach 100,000 miles?

2 **Extended Response** Donna wants to ride her bike at least 50 miles every week. At the beginning of the week the odometer on her bike showed 143.6 miles. Now it shows she has ridden 184.8 miles.

  a. How many more miles does she have to ride this week to meet her goal?

  b. After this week, how many weeks will it take for her odometer to show 300 miles? Explain how you found your answer.

3 Steve started with $25.81. Last week he spent $7.50, and he earned $12.75 washing cars. How much money does he have now?

4 A movie ticket costs $7.25.

  a. How much will 2 tickets cost?

  b. What will the change be if the 2 tickets were paid for with a $20 bill?

  c. How much will 4 tickets cost?

5 Melissa needs 6 pounds of cheese to make queso dip for her party. She bought a package of cheese that weighs 2.2 pounds and one that weighs 2.6 pounds.

  a. How many more pounds of cheese does she need? What number sentences did you use to solve the problem?

  b. If she buys another package of cheese and it weighs 2.1 pounds, how much will be left over?

eTextbook This lesson is available in the *eTextbook*.

Harder Roll a Decimal Game

Players: Two

Materials: *Number Cubes:* one 0–5 (red), one 5–10 (blue)

Object: To get the greater total score

Math Focus: Place value, subtracting decimal numbers, and mathematical reasoning

HOW TO PLAY

❶ Follow rules 1 through 4 for the **Roll a Decimal Game** on page 397.

❷ Subtract the lesser decimal from the greater decimal, and award the difference to the player with the greater decimal.

❸ After an agreed upon number of rounds, add your scores.

❹ The player with the greater total is the winner.

SAMPLE GAME

Round	Devonte	Airlea	Devonte's score	Airlea's score
1	0.76	0.966		0.206
2	0.957	0.676	0.281	
3	0.97775	0.9665	0.01125	
4	0.8	0.9576		0.1576
5	0.99	0.866	0.124	
6	0.86855	0.8875		0.01895
		Total	0.41625	0.38255

After six rounds, Devonte was the winner.

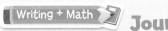 **Journal**

Create a word problem that involves using addition and subtraction of decimals to find the answer.

Balancing a Checkbook

Key Ideas

Adding and subtracting decimals is useful in practical applications, such as balancing a checkbook.

Many people keep money in personal checking accounts. They use addition and subtraction after each transaction to record how much money they have in their account.

Whenever Ms. Taylor pays with a check or debit card, or makes a withdrawal from her checking account, she keeps a record of the transaction in her checkbook register. This helps her keep track of how much money she has in her checking account.

Ms. Taylor keeps the record of each transaction in a check register. Look at this check register to see what information is on it.

CHECK	DATE	TRANSACTION	DEBIT	CREDIT	BALANCE
					907 13
				649 39	+ 649 39
D	1-3-06	Deposit			1556 52
			475 00		− 475 00
109	1-3	Star Realty Co. Rent			1081 52

Solve the following.

1 Why did Ms. Taylor use a *D* in the Check column?

2 What does the word *debit* mean?

3 How much was Ms. Taylor's deposit on February 21, 2006?

4 On what date was Ms. Taylor's only deposit made?

e Textbook This lesson is available in the *eTextbook*.

Every month Ms. Taylor gets a statement from her bank. The statement shows the bank's records of her account.

Her statement for January said that Ms. Taylor had $907.13 in her account on January 3, and $1,345.61 at the end of the month. This did not agree with her records.

CHECK	DATE	TRANSACTION	DEBIT		CREDIT		BALANCE	
							907	13
D	1-3	Deposit			649	39	+ 649	39
							1556	52
109	1-3	Star Realty Co. Rent	475	00			− 475	00
							1081	52
ATM	1-8	CASH	50	00			− 50	00
							1031	52
110	1-12	Watts Power Co. electricity	83	19			− 83	19
							1114	71
111	1-14	Betty's Boutique Pants	34	26			− 34	26
							1080	45
112	1-16	Clothing Mart Jacket	110	85			− 110	85
							969	60
113	1-28	Terrific Travel Agency bus tickets	107	00			− 107	00
							862	60
D	1-30	Deposit			649	39	+ 649	39
							1511	99

Refer to Ms. Taylor's checkbook register above to solve the following problem.

5 Did Ms. Taylor make an error in her calculations? If she did, correct the error and all following entries so that her records show the same balance at the end of the month as the bank statement shows.

6 If Ms. Taylor's new balance is $1345.61 and the next transaction is her rent for February, what will her new balance be? (Assume the rent has not increased or decreased since January.)

7 On February 6, Ms. Taylor received a check in the mail from Watts Power Company stating that she had overpaid on her gas and electric bill. Ms. Taylor deposited the check for $23.78 into her checking account. What is her new balance?

Solve each problem.

8 Karen opened a new checking account with $150. She wrote a check for $57.14 to pay her satellite television bill. Then she wrote a check for $67.09 to pay for groceries. Does she have enough money left in her checking account to withdraw $30 in cash?

9 Dr. Xiang made a deposit of $215.81 to her checking account. That gave her a balance of $403.05. How much money did Dr. Xiang have in her account before she made the deposit?

10 Jared wrote a check in the amount of $28.46 for two CDs. He wrote another check for $42.69 to pay for a new sweatshirt. Jared's original balance was $116.39. What is his new balance?

11 Michael had $507.08 in his checking account. He made a deposit for $325.00 and then wrote one check for $106.88 and another check for $75. What is his new balance?

12 Yesterday Phillipe wrote a check for $18.45. This morning he withdrew $40.00. His new balance is $97.88.

  a. What was his balance before both of these transactions?

  b. If Phillipe wants to bring his new balance to $100, how much money should he deposit into his checking account?

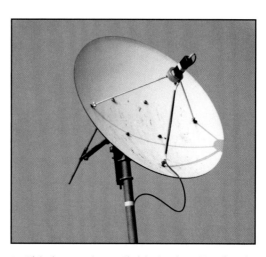

eTextbook This lesson is available in the *eTextbook*.

When writing entries in his checkbook, Bill always rounds the entries by dropping the cents. For example, when he needs to make a payment of $43.98, he records $43 as the amount for the check in his checkbook. Bill would record a deposit to his account of $97.01 as $97.

13 **Extended Response** Because Bill does this both for deposits to his account and for checks he writes, he thinks that his account should balance out in the end. Do you think it should? Why or why not?

One month Bill made deposits in the following amounts: $416.20, $416.20, and $98.80.

He also wrote checks in the following amounts: $7.83, $59.46, $12.50, $25.00, $241.10, $17.69, $50.00, $28.54, $25.00, $16.58, $57.43, $247.56, $73.12, $57.34, and $10.00.

14 Assume Bill started with a balance of $100 in his checking account.

a. What should his balance be at the end of the month?

b. What would Bill think his balance is?

15 If Bill continues this process for the entire year, what problem situations might he encounter?

Journal

Explain why it is a good idea to record transactions in a checkbook.

Multiplying by a Whole Number

Key Ideas

You can use what you know about place value and multiplying whole numbers and decimals.

Jenny is making 21 flags for her school's Color Guard. Each flag takes 1.3 meters of cloth. What is the total length of cloth Jenny needs?

To find out, you would multiply 1.3 by 21.

Chad told Jenny that 1.3×21 was 27.3.

Can that be right? Why or why not?

You could do the problem using decimeters. Multiply 13 by 21.

```
    13
  × 21
 ─────
    13
   26
 ─────
   273
```

273 dm = 27.3 m

So Jenny needs 27.3 meters of cloth. Chad was right.
$21 \times 1.3 = 27.3$

Let's look at the two multiplications side by side.

```
    13          1.3
  × 21        × 21
 ─────       ─────
    13          13
   26          26
 ─────       ─────
   273         27.3
```

The problems and the answers are the same except for the decimal point.

Can you figure out a simple rule for deciding where to put the decimal point in the answer?

ⓔ Textbook This lesson is available in the *eTextbook*.

To multiply a decimal by a whole number:

1. Estimate the product.
2. Multiply as you would with two whole numbers.
3. Put the decimal point in the answer as many places from the right as it is in the decimal factor.

Example 1: 514 × 2.3

If we estimate the product we know the answer will be between 1,000 (500 × 2) and 1,800 (600 × 3).

```
    5 1 4    Multiply as you would with two whole numbers.
  × 2.3
   1542
 + 1028
  1182.2    The decimal point is one place from the right.
            So, place the decimal point one place from the
            right in the answer.
```

Example 2: 0.24 × 79

If we estimate the product, we know the answer will be approximately 20 (estimate about 25% of 80).

```
   0.24    Multiply as you would with two whole numbers.
  ×  79
    216
 +  168
  18.96    The decimal point is two places from the right in
           0.24. So, in the answer, place the decimal point
           two places from the right.
```

Estimate the product, then multiply.

1. 3.07 × 11

2. 0.83 × 22

3. 7,198 × 0.09

4. 385 × 1.2

5. 82 × 0.03

6. 97.8 × 79

7. 6.8 × 13

8. 39 × 2.25

9. 2.36 × 1,528

10. 0.25 × 12

Remember, if we estimate the product we know the answer will be between 40 (4 × 10) and 100 (5 × 20).

$$
\begin{array}{r}
4.0\,7 \\
\times\ 1\,2 \\
\hline
8\,1\,4 \\
+\ 4\,0\,7 \\
\hline
4\,8.8\,4
\end{array}
$$

4.0 7 The decimal point is two places from the right.

4 8.8 4 Place the decimal point two places from the right.

Estimate the product, then multiply.

11 256 × 1.2

12 617 × 2.5

13 451 × 82.3

14 112 × 4.92

15 673 × 5.6

Solve these problems.

16 Bart is the manager of a baseball team. His team needs 13 new shirts. Each shirt costs $7.29. Bart has $75.

   a. Does he have enough money?

   b. If not, how much more money does Bart need?

17 Myrna wants to buy 2 shelves. One is 3 meters long, and the other is 4 meters long. Each shelf costs $4.05 per meter. How much will the 2 shelves cost?

18 **Extended Response** Mr. Washington is building a house. He needs 27 electrical outlets. Each outlet costs $2.71. Will the 27 outlets cost more than $100 altogether? Explain how you found your answer.

19 The Omega Publishing Company ships an average of 751 books each week. It costs 48¢ to mail each book. How much does mailing cost, on average, each week?

20 Eric needs to buy stamps to send 21 party invitations. Each stamp costs 37¢. Eric has $7.75. Does he have enough money to buy stamps for all of the invitations?

Writing + Math Journal

Will the product of a decimal number less than one and a whole number be greater than or less than the original numbers? Why? Give an example to support your answer.

Textbook This lesson is available in the *eTextbook*.

Decimal Roll a Problem Game

Players: Two

Materials: *Number Cube:* one 0–5 (red)

Object: To get the greatest product

Math Focus: Multiplication of one- and two-digit decimal numbers and whole numbers, place value, and mathematical reasoning.

HOW TO PLAY

1 Use blanks to outline a multiplication problem on your paper, like this:

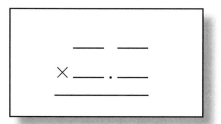

2 The first player will roll the **Number Cube** four times.

3 Each time the **Number Cube** is rolled, write that number in one of the blanks on your outline.

4 When all of the blanks have been filled in, find the product of the two numbers.

5 The player with the greatest product wins the round.

Other Ways To Play the Game:

• Try to get the least product.

• Move the decimal so the second number is a decimal number in the hundredths place.

• Use a 5–10 **Number Cube**. If you roll a 10, roll again.

Key Ideas

Points with decimal coordinates can be shown on a graph.

Solve these problems. Draw and complete the charts.

1 Use the function rule to complete the chart.

$x \to \boxed{\times 3} \to \boxed{-2} \to y$

x	y
1	1
2	4
3	▪
4	▪
5	▪

2 Now plot the points on a sheet of graph paper.

3 Do all five points seem to be on the same straight line?

4 Fill in the following chart for the function rule in Problem 1. Then plot all of these points on the same graph you used for Problem 2. Do these points also seem to lie on the same straight line?

x	y
1.1	1.3
1.2	1.6
1.3	▪
1.9	▪
2.3	▪
2.6	▪
3.2	▪
3.7	▪
4.1	▪
4.5	▪
4.8	▪
4.9	▪

e Textbook This lesson is available in the *eTextbook*.

"I've got another idea," said Ahmal, as he drew a line on the map from the tree to the rock. "All I have to do is write down how big this angle is," he said. "Then whoever reads the directions can stand at the rock, look at the tree, turn the correct amount to the right, walk seven meters, and dig."

How can Ahmal write down how big the angle is?

Ahmal thought about how to describe the size of the angle. "If I stand on the rock, face the tree, and then turn completely around, I will be facing the tree again. If I turn one-half of the way around, I will be facing directly away from the tree. If I turn one-quarter of the way around, I still will have passed the point where I would be facing the treasure. I think I would be facing the treasure if I just turned about one-sixth of the way around."

Ahmal wrote,

> "Stand on the big rock. Look at the closest tree. Turn to your right (or clockwise) until you have made $\frac{1}{6}$ of a complete turn. Walk 7 meters. Dig."

2 **Extended Response** Is this enough information? Explain.

An angle that is "one-fourth of a complete turn" is called a right angle. These are right angles:

 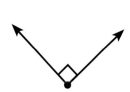 

An angle that is less than a right angle is called an acute angle. These are acute angles:

An angle that is more than a right angle (but less than half of a complete turn) is called an obtuse angle. These are obtuse angles:

3 **Extended Response** What kind of an angle is $\frac{1}{6}$ of a complete turn? Explain your answer.

e Textbook This lesson is available in the *eTextbook*.

Each angle below is labeled with a letter at the corner of the angle.

The corner of the angle is called the vertex. The two intersecting lines, rays, or line segments that make the angle are called the *sides of the angle.*

Tell whether each angle is an acute angle, a right angle, or an obtuse angle.

4

5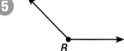

6

7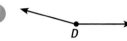

8

9

10 **Extended Response** Explain an easy way to describe the difference between acute, obtuse and right angles to another student.

Use your protractor to measure these angles.

11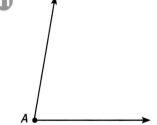

12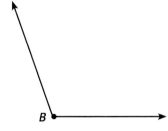

13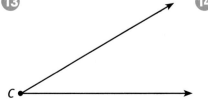

14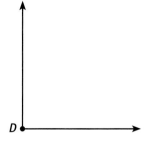

> **Writing + Math**
>
> **Journal**
> Explain how fractional turns are related to angles, and provide two examples of fractional turns as angles.

Key Ideas

Two lines in the same plane are either parallel or intersecting. Some intersecting lines are perpendicular.

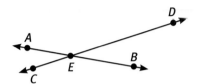

Intersecting lines are lines that meet. In this figure, lines *AB* and *CD* intersect at point *E*.

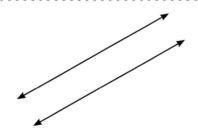

Parallel lines are lines that go in the same direction. The lines in this figure are parallel lines. Parallel lines never meet. They remain the same distance apart no matter how far they are extended.

Two lines are perpendicular if they meet to form right angles.

These lines are perpendicular.

Answer the following questions.

1. Try to draw two lines that meet to form one right angle and three other angles that are not right angles. The two lines must be straight and must continue through the point where they meet. Can you do it?

2. If two lines meet so that one angle formed is a right angle, what kind of angles will the other three angles be?

3. Draw two capital letters from the alphabet that demonstrate intersecting line segments.

e Textbook This lesson is available in the *eTextbook*.

In each case, tell whether the two lines are perpendicular or not perpendicular.

④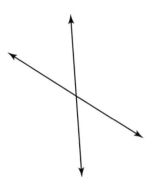

⑤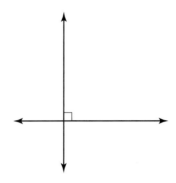

⑥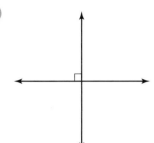

⑦

In each case, tell whether the two lines are parallel, perpendicular, or neither.

⑧

⑨

⑩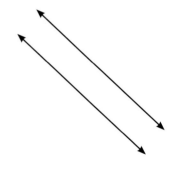

⑪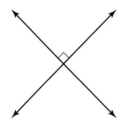

⑫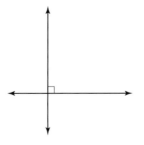

⑬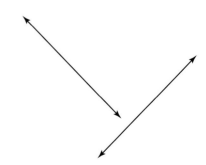

⑭ Draw a line. Now draw two more lines, each perpendicular to the first. What do you think is true of these last two lines?

Quadrilaterals and Other Polygons

Key Ideas

A polygonal region includes the inside of a plane figure. A polygon is the line segments that form the polygonal region.

All the figures shown are called polygons. A polygon is a figure in a plane with three or more line segments as sides (*poly-* in Greek means "many").

A polygon with five sides is called a pentagon (*penta-* in Greek means "five"). A polygon with six sides is a hexagon (*hexa-* in Greek means "six"). A polygon with eight sides is an octagon (*octa-* in Greek means "eight").

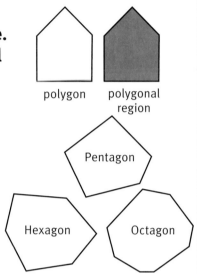

polygon   polygonal region

Pentagon

Hexagon   Octagon

Four-sided polygons are called quadrilaterals (which in Latin means "four sides"). Some quadrilaterals have special names. A square, a rectangle, a trapezoid, a parallelogram, and a rhombus are all special quadrilaterals.

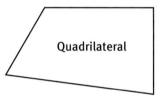

Quadrilateral

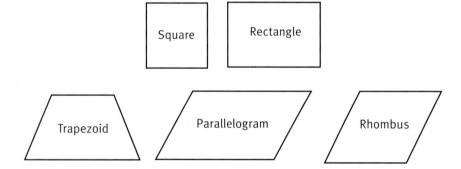

Square

Rectangle

Trapezoid

Parallelogram

Rhombus

ⓔ**Textbook** This lesson is available in the *eTextbook*.

Draw the following.

1 Draw an octagon.

2 Draw a pentagon.

3 Draw a hexagon.

4 Draw a quadrilateral with two of its sides parallel but the other two sides not parallel.

5 Draw a quadrilateral with two pairs of parallel sides.

6 Draw a quadrilateral with two pairs of parallel sides and all sides of the same length.

7 Draw a quadrilateral with two pairs of parallel sides and all angles of the same size.

8 Draw a quadrilateral with two pairs of parallel sides and all sides and angles of the same size.

9 **Extended Response** What is the difference between the parallelogram and the rectangle on page 456?

10 **Extended Response** What is the difference between the square and the rhombus on page 456?

Writing + Math

Journal

Create a shape containing only three pairs of parallel sides. Explain how you found your answer.

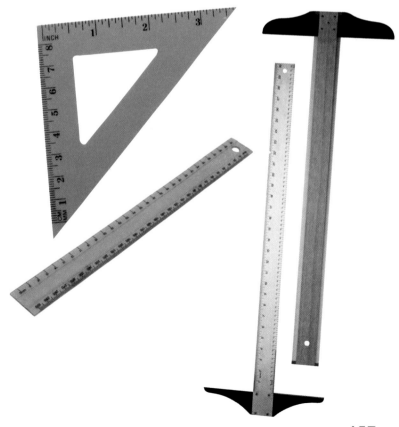

Key Ideas

A polygon that has three sides is called a *triangle*. There are different types of triangles.

 equilateral triangle—all three sides are equal in length

 isosceles triangle—two sides are equal in length

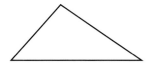 **scalene triangle**—all the sides have a different length

 right triangle—a triangle with a right angle

 acute triangle—a triangle with three acute angles

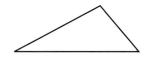 **obtuse triangle**—a triangle with one obtuse angle

eTextbook This lesson is available in the *eTextbook*.

Decide whether each net would make a cube. Compare your answers with those of your classmates. If you disagree, the person who thinks it is possible should show that it will make a cube.

5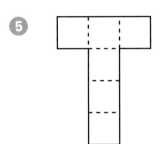

6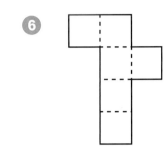

7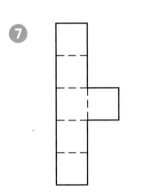

8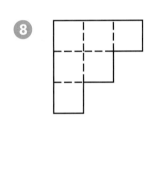

9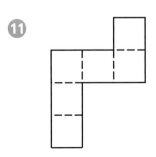

10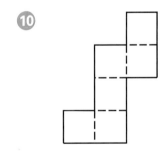

11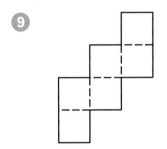

12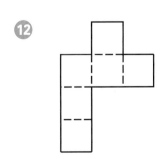

Key Ideas

Every polyhedron is made up of polygons joined together to form a closed surface.

For example, a cube is made from six squares, each with four corners and four sides. This figure shows how we will refer to the parts of the polygons in the plane and to the parts of the polyhedra in space.

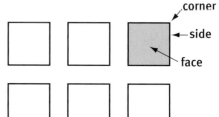

corner
side
face

When the six faces are put together to make a cube, the places where two sides meet are called *edges*. The place where the corners meet is called a *vertex* (the plural of vertex is vertices). The polygons themselves are called *faces*. The cube is actually hollow.

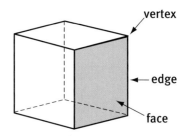

vertex
edge
face

e Textbook This lesson is available in the *eTextbook*.

There are only five regular polyhedra. These regular polyhedra are also known as platonic solids, although they are actually hollow. In a regular polyhedron, all the faces are regular polygons, and the same number of polygons meet at each vertex. For example, the dodecahedron is made up of twelve regular pentagons, and three pentagons meet at each vertex. The icosahedron is made up of twenty equilateral triangles, and five triangles meet at each vertex.

The Platonic Solids

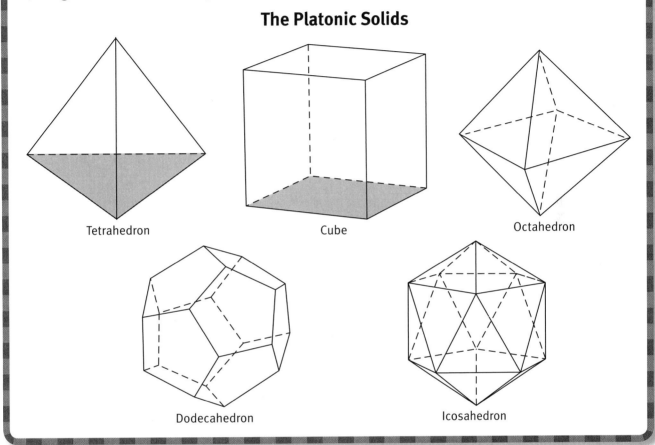

Tetrahedron   Cube   Octahedron

Dodecahedron   Icosahedron

Answer these questions.

1. How many triangles does it take to make a tetrahedron?

2. How many triangles meet at each vertex of a tetrahedron?

3. How many squares does it take to make a cube?

4. How many squares meet at each vertex of a cube?

5. How many triangles does it take to make an octahedron?

6. How many triangles meet at each vertex of an octahedron?

Use models of regular polyhedra to complete the table and the questions that follow it. Look for patterns.

V = number of vertices E = number of edges F = number of faces

7

Name of Polyhedron	Illustration of Model	V	E	F
Tetrahedron				
Cube				
Octahedron				
Dodecahedron		20	30	
Icosahedron			30	20

8 Look at your completed table.

a. What do you notice about the entries for *V, E,* and *F* for the entire table? Express this as an equation.

b. **Extended Response** What do you notice about the entries for *V, E,* and *F* for both the dodecahedron and the icosahedron? For both the cube and octahedron?

Put a regular tetrahedron on the desk and [...] down at a vertex. It should look like this:

This means you can rotate a regular tetrahedron $\frac{1}{3}$ of a turn and it will look the same as before you rotated it. You could also rotate it $\frac{2}{3}$ of a turn.

Complete the following.

9 Set a cube on a table and draw what you see when you look straight down at it.

10 How much can you rotate the cube so that it still looks the same as before you rotated it?

11 Set a decahedron on a table and draw what you see if you look straight down at it.

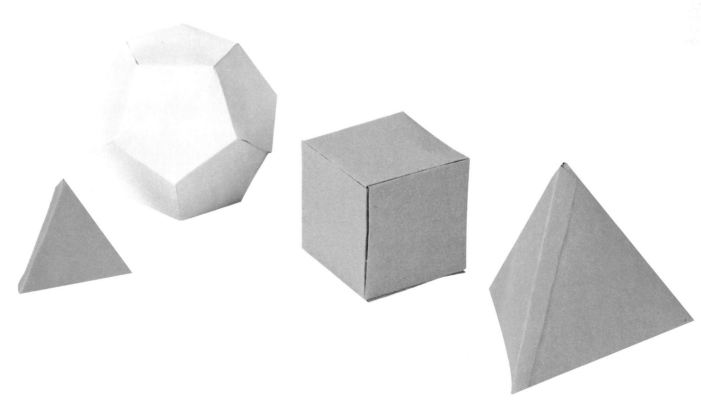

Ke and prisms can have any polygon as their base.

Triangular Pyramid

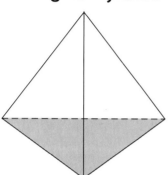

Square Pyramid

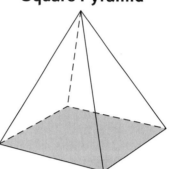

Pentagonal Pyramid

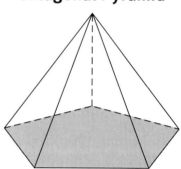

If you were going to make a square pyramid, you would need the following polygons:

How many faces, edges, and vertices does a square pyramid have? It has five faces, eight edges, and five vertices. How many sides are there in all the polygons that make up a square pyramid? There are sixteen sides.

Answer the following questions.

1 Draw the polygons you would need to construct a pentagonal pyramid.

2 How many faces does the pentagonal pyramid have?

3 How many sides are there in all these polygons?

4 How many edges does the pentagonal pyramid have?

5 How many vertices does the pentagonal pyramid have?

ⓔ **Textbook** This lesson is available in the *eTextbook.*

A *prism* is a space figure with two parallel, congruent bases. Here are some net diagrams that produce prisms.

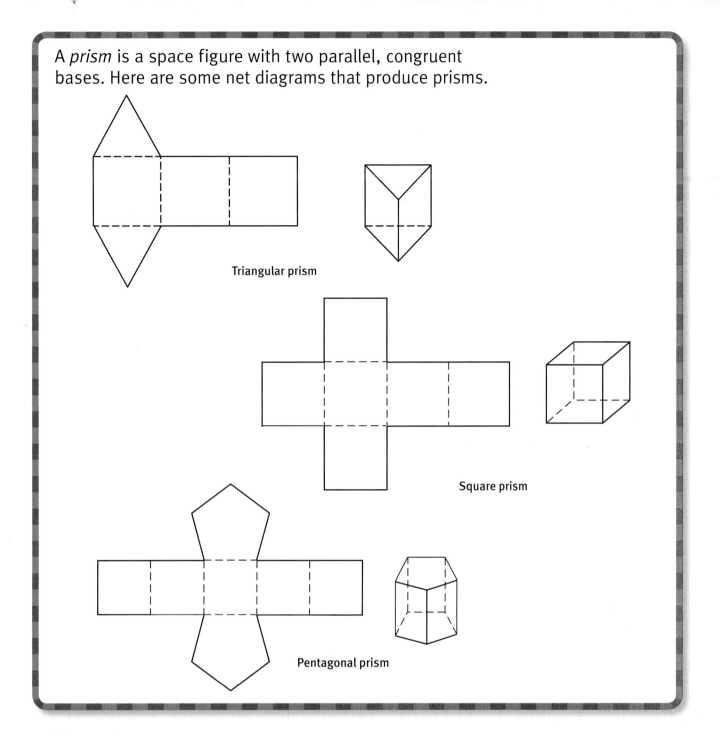

Triangular prism

Square prism

Pentagonal prism

Examine a triangular prism.

6 How many faces does the triangular prism have?

7 How many sides are there altogether in these polygons?

8 How many edges does the triangular prism have?

9 How many corners do these polygons have altogether?

10 How many vertices does the triangular prism have?

Answer the following questions.

11 How many faces does the pentagonal prism have?

12 How many sides are there altogether in the polygons that form the pentagonal prism?

13 How many edges does the pentagonal prism have?

14 How many corners do the polygons that form the pentagonal prism have altogether?

15 How many vertices does the pentagonal prism have?

Use models to fill in the tables below and answer the questions. Look for patterns. Remember that V = number of vertices, E = number of edges, and F = number of faces.

16

Name of Polyhedron	Illustration of Model	V	E	F
Triangular Pyramid				
Square Pyramid				
Pentagonal Pyramid				

17 If you continue to increase the number of sides of the bases by one, what would you expect the values of V, E, and F to be?

18 What is another name for a triangular pyramid?

Fill in the table, and answer the questions below.
Look for patterns.

⑲

Name of Polyhedron	Illustration of Model	V	E	F
Triangular Prism		⬜	⬜	⬜
Square Prism		⬜	⬜	⬜
Pentagonal Prism		⬜	⬜	⬜

⑳ If you continue to increase the number of sides of the bases by one, what would you expect the next number to be for *V*? For *E*? For *F*?

㉑ If you continue to increase the number of sides of the bases, what will a prism "look" like?

Answer these questions.

㉒ What is the relationship between the vertices, edges, and faces of a pyramid or prism?

㉓ Which models can be rotated $\frac{1}{3}$ of a turn and still look the same?

㉔ Which models can be rotated $\frac{1}{4}$ of a turn and still look the same?

㉕ Which models can be rotated $\frac{1}{5}$ of a turn and still look the same?

Calculating Area

Key Ideas

You can calculate the area of a figure by counting squares and parts of squares on a grid.

Each square has an area of 1 square centimeter. The area of the shaded rectangle is 21 square centimeters.

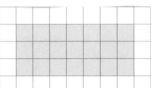

You can also calculate the area of the rectangle by multiplying the length by the width. The length is 7 centimeters and the width is 3 centimeters. So the area is 21 square centimeters.

Look at the figure below.

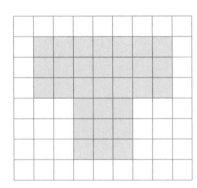

Calculate the area of this shaded shape by counting the number of squares. Did you count 30 squares?

What would you do if you could not count squares? You do not know how to find the area of such a figure. But, you do know how to find the area of a rectangle and of a square. Try breaking the figure into smaller parts.

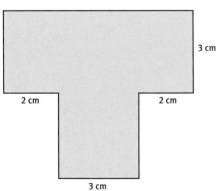

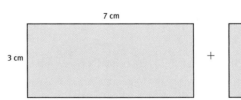

Rectangle
A = length $\times$ width
A = 7 cm $\times$ 3 cm
A = 21 square cm

Square
A = side $\times$ side
A = 3 cm $\times$ 3 cm
A = 9 square cm

Area of the shaded figure = 21 square cm + 9 square cm = 30 square cm

e Textbook This lesson is available in the *eTextbook.*

Find the area of each figure.

1

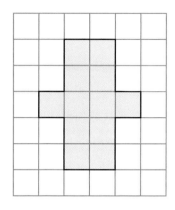

2

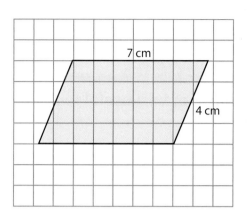

7 cm
4 cm

Estimate the area of the figures.

3

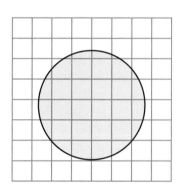

4

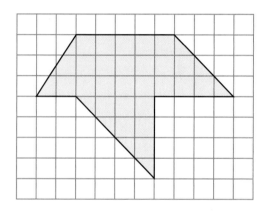

Find the area. Assume that if a figure looks like a square or a rectangle, then it is.

5

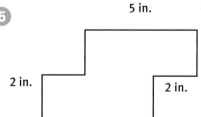

5 in.
2 in.
2 in.

6

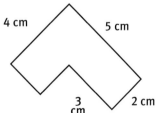

4 cm   5 cm
3 cm   2 cm

7

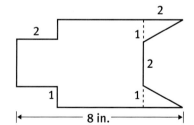

2   2
2   1
1   2
1   1
8 in.

8 **Extended Response** In Problem 4, can you divide the large figure into smaller figures? Explain why or why not. If it is possible, estimate the area of each of the smaller figures using the grid.

Key Ideas

A grid can be a useful tool for finding the perimeter of an object.

Remember that *perimeter* is the distance around a figure. Look at the figure below. What is the perimeter?

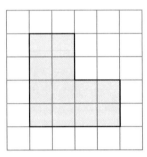

Count the sides of the squares that make the boundary of the figure. Since you are solving for perimeter, you count *around* the figure.

The perimeter of this figure is 16 units.

You can also find the perimeter of a rectangle if you know its area and the length of one of its sides.

5 units

For example, the area of this rectangle is 35 square centimeters, and the length of one side is 5 centimeters. What number multiplied by 5 equals 35? The length of the other side is 7 centimeters. Now that you know the length of the sides of the rectangle, you can find the perimeter.

P = 7 + 5 + 7 + 5 = 24 units

Textbook This lesson is available in the *eTextbook*.

Find the perimeter of each figure. Each square on the graph paper represents one centimeter on each side.

1.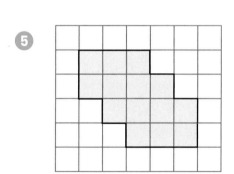

2.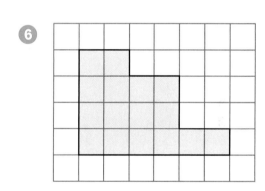

3.

4.

5.

6.

7. If a square has an area of 49 square meters, what is its perimeter?

8. If you know one of the sides of a rectangle is 9 centimeters, and its area is 27 square centimeters, what is its perimeter?

9. Can rectangles that have the same area have different perimeters?

10. Can rectangles that have the same perimeter have different areas?

 **Journal**

How many different rectangles have a perimeter of 24 units and side lengths that are whole units? Which has the greatest area?

Not Seeing Is Believing

In 1820, there was only one way for people who are blind to read. Each letter of the alphabet was raised from the page so it could be felt with the fingers. This might sound simple, but it was not. The Qs felt like Os. The Os felt like Cs. The Is turned out to be Ts, and the Rs were really Bs.

Louis Braille, who was blind, was one of the brightest boys in his school. But often even he forgot the beginning of a sentence before he got to the end of it. It would take months to read a single book this way!

One day in 1821, Captain Charles Barbier came to Louis's school. Captain Barbier had worked out a way for his soldiers to use raised dots to send messages in the dark. In his night-writing system, a different pattern of dots represented each sound. The dots were pushed into heavy sheets of paper with a long, pointed tool called a stylus. When the paper was turned over, raised dots could be felt on the other side.

Portrait of Louis Braille

But there were so many sounds in the French language that it took almost a hundred dots to write out a simple word. Night-writing also took up far too much room. Most of all, it was hard to learn and to feel.

Night-writing might have worked well for notes on the battlefield, but it was no way to make books for the blind. Did that mean the dots were a failure? Louis did not think so.

ⓔ **Textbook** This lesson is available in the *eTextbook*.

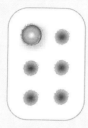

L ouis decided he was going to work out a way for the blind to *really* read and write with dots. He tried not to waste a single minute. Even on vacation, he worked on his dots.

Three years went by. Sometimes Louis got so tired he could hardly lift his hand. Again and again, he simplified Captain Barbier's pattern of dots. But still they were not simple enough.

Then Louis had a very different idea. What if he used dots in a new way— not to stand for sounds, but to stand for letters?

First Louis took a pencil and marked six dots on a heavy piece of paper. Then he took his stylus and raised one of the dots.

That would stand for the letter *a*. Louis made letter after letter. And when he was finished, Louis Braille's alphabet of dots looked like the illustration below.

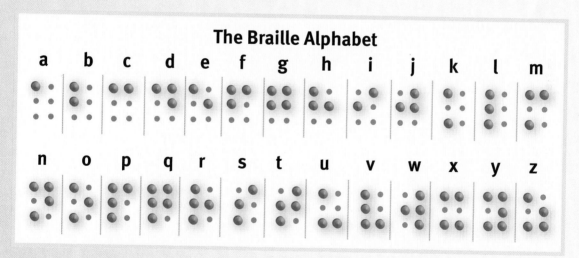

The Braille Alphabet

a b c d e f g h i j k l m

n o p q r s t u v w x y z

Edited excerpts from *Louis Braille: The Boy Who Invented Books for the Blind*.

1. Why do you think that only one letter is made with a single dot?

2. Why wouldn't a system based on a grid of four dots instead of six dots work?

Exploring Problem Solving

You can write messages in braille by making dots with a pencil on grid paper. Press hard. Turn the paper over.

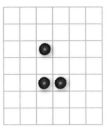

Be careful. What happens to the pattern of dots when you flip the page? Try making the letter *u* in braille to find out.

Solve these problems.

3. In the regular alphabet, which lowercase letters will stay the same when you flip the page?

4. In the regular alphabet, which lowercase letters will become a different letter when you flip the page?

5. In the braille alphabet, which letters will become a different letter when you flip the page?

6. Suppose you flip the page as shown here, so it is around a horizontal line instead of around a vertical line. Which braille letters will stay the same, and which will become different letters?

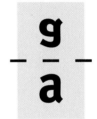